WHEN
FISH
GOT FEET,

WHEN BUGS WERE BIG,

EEK!

& WHEN DINOS DAWNED

A Cartoon Prehistory of Life on Earth

Hannah Bonner

NATIONAL GEOGRAPHIC

WASHINGTON, D.C.

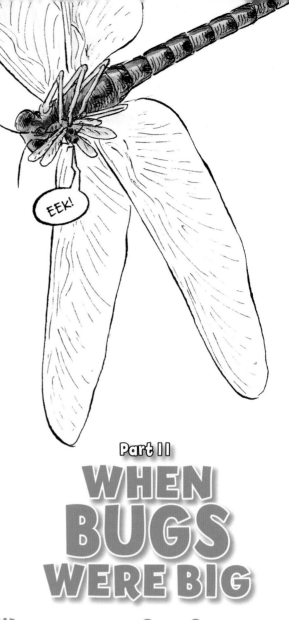

Part III

WHEN DINOS DAWNED

Dear Reader,

The book you're about to read (or skim, or flip through to check out the pictures) will take you on a journey that begins when life comes out of the seas and onto land, and ends just as the dinosaurs are beginning to take over the planet.

I didn't make up the plot. In fact, the plot was set in stone—the stone of the fossil record. But since reality is generally weirder than fiction, you can rest assured that this tale includes plenty of bizarre plants and animals, strange ecosystems, devastating extinctions, sharp fangs, dancing continents, and a bunch of silly cartoons. Granted, the latter are not exactly part of the fossil record, but I wanted to have fun writing the book, and I wanted you to have fun reading it.

The three sections in this book were originally three separate books. In putting them together, I've had a chance to update several scientific facts based on new discoveries, and to add some bonus pages at the end.

Enjoy!
Hannah Bonner

Hi there,

Thank you for choosing to read this book. It means that you are a clever and discerning human who realizes that dinosaurs were not the only interesting creatures on the planet, and that there were lots of us cool animals and plants that came before them. Not that I'm resentful or anything, I just think that dinosaurs get way too much attention. Plus, do you know who your ancestors were? We were! So I guess we didn't do too badly after all.

Carnivorous regards,

Arctognathus

PS: I'm afraid you'll have to put up with some dinosaurs in the last chapters of the book. Sorry!

Arctognathus, a reptile-like member of the therapsids, the group that gave rise to mammals

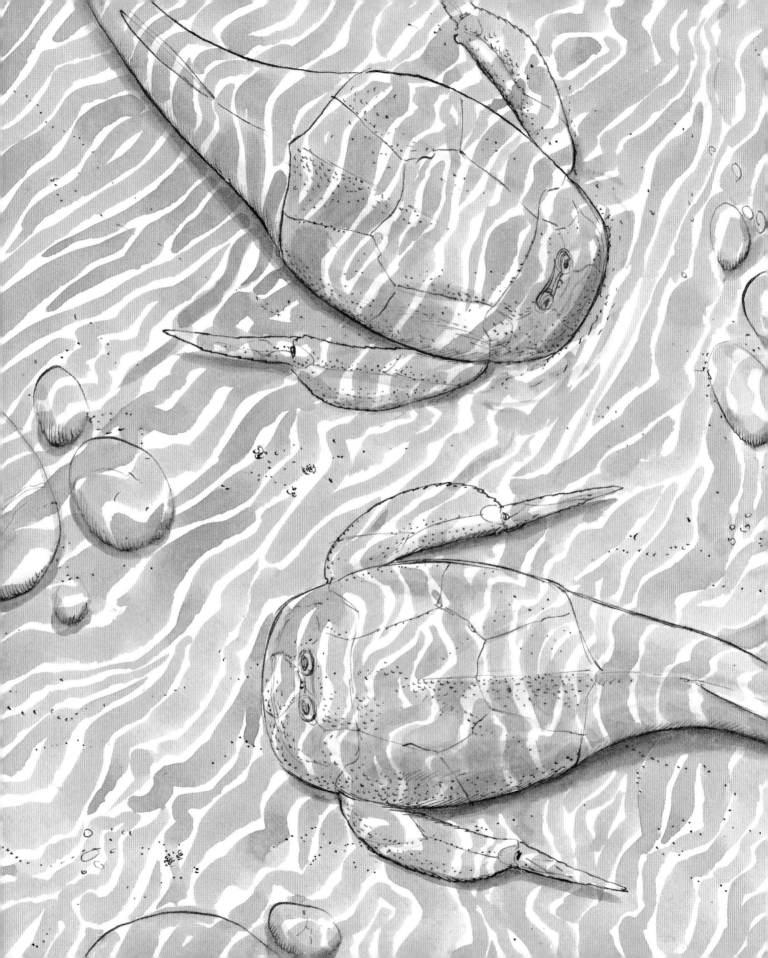

Part I

WHEN FISH GOT FEET, SHARKS GOT TEETH, & BUGS BEGAN TO SWARM

A Cartoon Prehistory of Life Long Before Dinosaurs

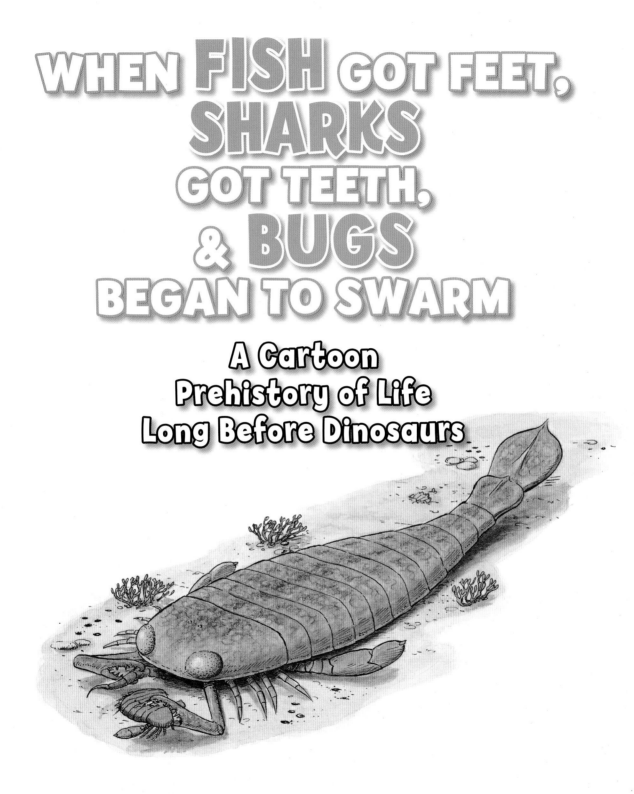

WELCOME TO PENNSYLVANIA

What, you don't recognize Pennsylvania? That's not surprising. Nowadays the countryside in Pennsylvania is covered in greenery, but 430 million years ago the tallest plants around would have been knee-high to a grasshopper, had there been any grasshoppers. There weren't. Instead there were some small millipedes and other bugs crawling around under equally tiny plants. There were moss relatives a few inches tall, lichens on the rocks, and slimy mats of algae and bacteria in the wetter spots. Mostly though, it was just rocks, rocks, and more rocks, with some gravel, sand, and silt thrown in for good measure.

AH, I DO LOVE THE FOREST!

FOREST? HA, HA, HA. TREES HAVEN'T EVOLVED YET. IT LOOKS LIKE A FOREST TO YOU 'CAUSE YOU'RE THE SIZE OF A PINHEAD.

Robin Mite and Friar Millipede stroll through Sherwood Moss Patch.

LOVELY, LIVELY SEA LIFE

Now let's take a look at the oceans. What a contrast with the barren-looking landscape we just saw! Life in the oceans was in high gear 430 million years ago.

A warm, shallow sea covered most of North America. In it, zillions of animals were busy eating algae, plankton, and one another.

In some places, such as what is now the Great Lakes region of the United States, reefs formed. Here's what Racine, Wisconsin, looked like back then.

GREAT SWIMMING WEATHER HERE IN WISCONSIN TODAY, FOLKS! WE'VE GOT A SUNNY 82° AND ALL THE PLANKTON YOU CAN EAT!

82°
86°

13

Who's Who on the Reef

Our modern reefs are made mostly of coral and algae. As you can see, coral was just one of many life-forms that built up these ancient reefs.

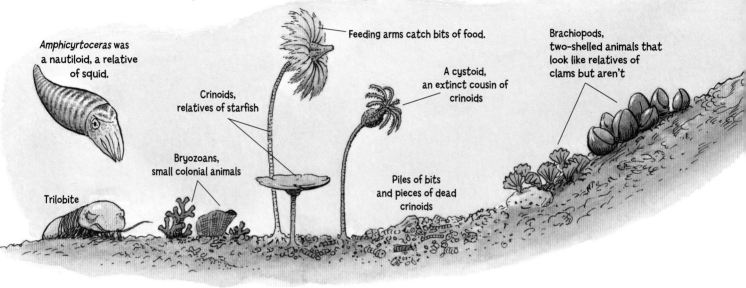

Amphicyrtoceras was a nautiloid, a relative of squid.

Feeding arms catch bits of food.

Brachiopods, two-shelled animals that look like relatives of clams but aren't

A cystoid, an extinct cousin of crinoids

Crinoids, relatives of starfish

Bryozoans, small colonial animals

Piles of bits and pieces of dead crinoids

Trilobite

Beyond the Reef

Of course there were all sorts of other watery environments besides reefs. Sandy and muddy bottoms were home to a variety of worms. The soft worms fell apart before they could fossilize, but we know they existed because the tunnels they made filled up with mud, which later turned to stone.

HMMM, WHAT HAVE WE HERE? FOSSILIZED SWISS CHEESE, PERHAPS? NO, IT'S TOO OLD. THESE MUST BE WORM BURROWS INSTEAD.

Algae, which didn't fossilize either but were probably common

Worm burrows

Carcinosoma

Two kinds of ancient coral, solitary and colonial

Dawsonoceras, another nautiloid, could be up to 3 ft (1 m) long.

A stromatoporoid, a kind of rocky sponge that helped build the reef

The top predators at this time were eurypterids, extinct relatives of scorpions. Most eurypterids were small, but a few were more than six feet (1.8 m) long. One of these giants was *Pterygotus,* seen here snacking on an unlucky fellow eurypterid called *Carcinosoma.*

In Deep Water

Out in the open ocean, the most common animals were very small creatures called graptolites, which lived in colonies. They floated slowly through the water, catching tiny plankton along the way.

Pterygotus

Close-up of a bit of a graptolite colony

Individual graptolite animal

Graptolite colony, life-size

AND WHERE, YOU MAY ASK, WERE THE FISH?

MIRROR, MIRROR, IN THE SEA, WHY DO I LOOK SO TURNIPY?

Good question! Actually, fish did exist back then, but they were small and not very common, and they usually lived near the shore, not the reef. Fish were the first vertebrates, or animals with backbones. Fossil fish scales date back more than 500 million years. The earliest fish were basic, no-frills models. They had a tail but no top or side fins to help them steer properly, so they must have been fairly slow and clumsy. These ancient fish didn't even have jaws. They did have a mouth, which they used to eat very small bits of food.

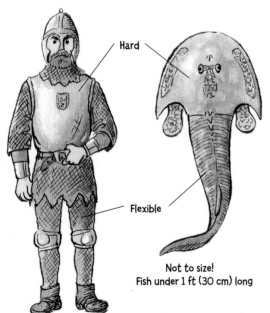

Hard

Flexible

Not to size!
Fish under 1 ft (30 cm) long

Unlike modern vertebrates, most early fish had more bones on the outside than on the inside, forming an armored box around them. Jawless fish had their heyday in the period of time called the Silurian. In the following period, the Devonian, fish with jaws gradually took over.

Only two kinds of jawless fish are still alive today: lampreys and hagfishes. Both look very different from their Silurian ancestors. Lampreys suck blood from living fish, and hagfishes are deep-water scavengers and worm-eaters. Hagfishes secrete gobs of sticky mucus when bothered, and their table manners consist of climbing into dead or dying fish and eating them from the inside out. Dee-lightful!

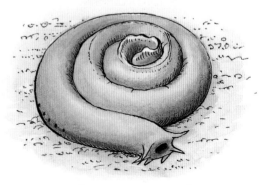

A hagfish, curled up on the seafloor

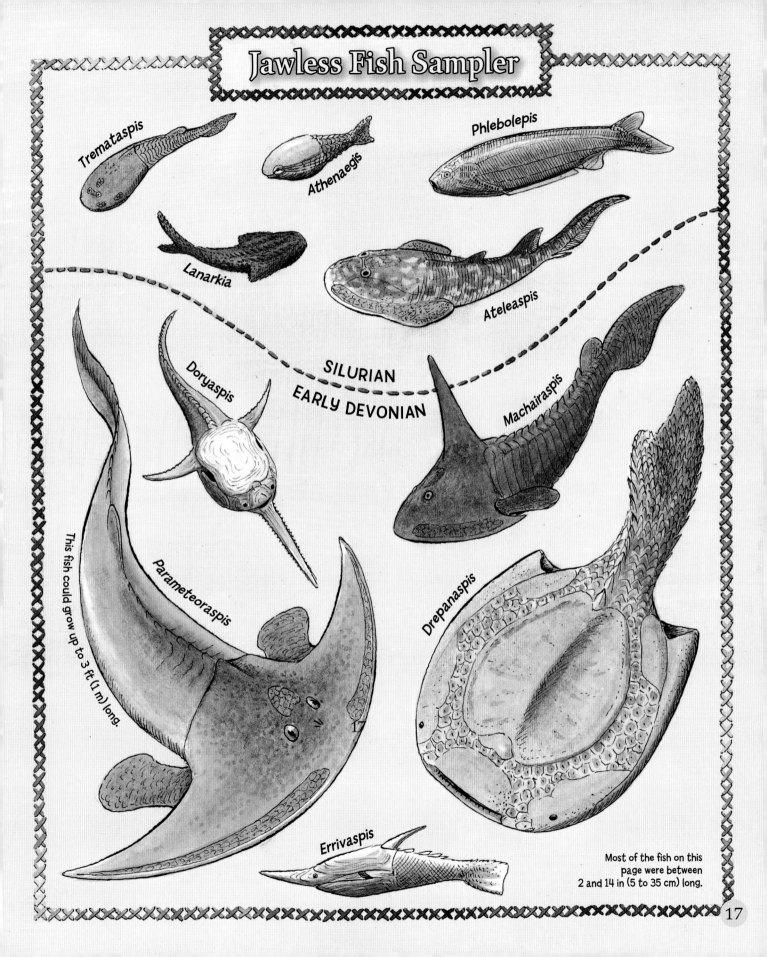

Jawless Fish Sampler

Tremataspis

Athenaegis

Phlebolepis

Lanarkia

Ateleaspis

Doryaspis

SILURIAN

EARLY DEVONIAN

Machairaspis

This fish could grow up to 3 ft (1 m) long.

Parameteoraspis

Drepanaspis

Errivaspis

Most of the fish on this page were between 2 and 14 in (5 to 35 cm) long.

THE SILURIAN PLANET

In the 19th century, a British scientist by the name of Murchison found many fossils in Wales that seemed to belong to the same prehistoric time period. He called this period the Silurian after the Silures, a fierce Celtic tribe that lived in Wales in Roman times. Of course, there were no Romans, Silures, or anyone else around 430 million years ago. Instead, Wales was underwater, just like Wisconsin.

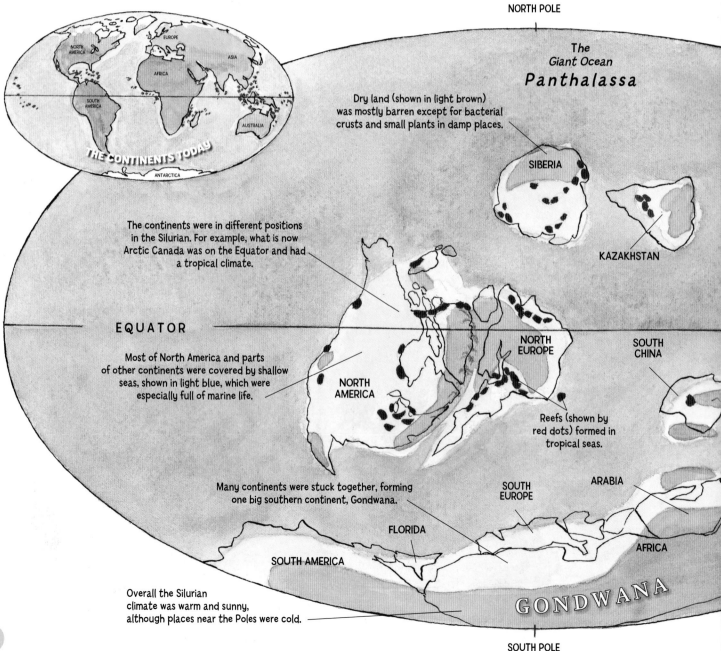

NORTH POLE

THE CONTINENTS TODAY

NORTH AMERICA
EUROPE
ASIA
AFRICA
SOUTH AMERICA
AUSTRALIA
ANTARCTICA

The
Giant Ocean
Panthalassa

Dry land (shown in light brown) was mostly barren except for bacterial crusts and small plants in damp places.

SIBERIA

KAZAKHSTAN

The continents were in different positions in the Silurian. For example, what is now Arctic Canada was on the Equator and had a tropical climate.

EQUATOR

Most of North America and parts of other continents were covered by shallow seas, shown in light blue, which were especially full of marine life.

NORTH AMERICA

NORTH EUROPE

SOUTH CHINA

Reefs (shown by red dots) formed in tropical seas.

SOUTH EUROPE

ARABIA

AFRICA

Many continents were stuck together, forming one big southern continent, Gondwana.

FLORIDA

SOUTH AMERICA

Overall the Silurian climate was warm and sunny, although places near the Poles were cold.

GONDWANA

SOUTH POLE

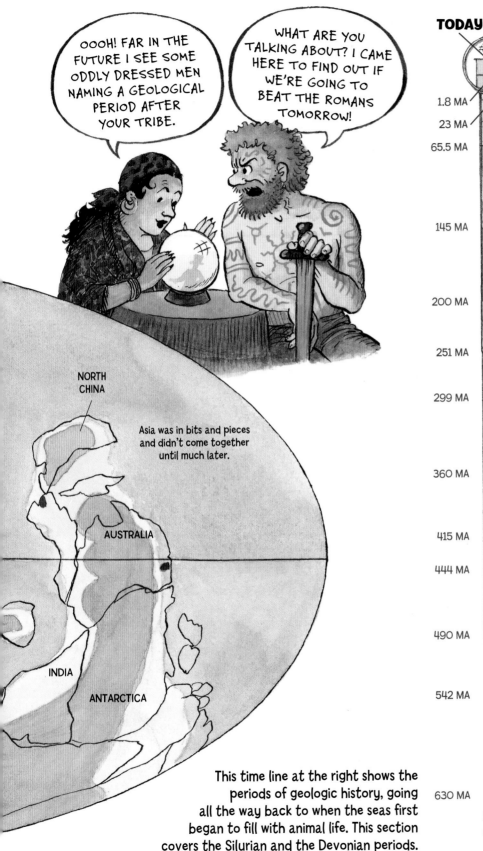

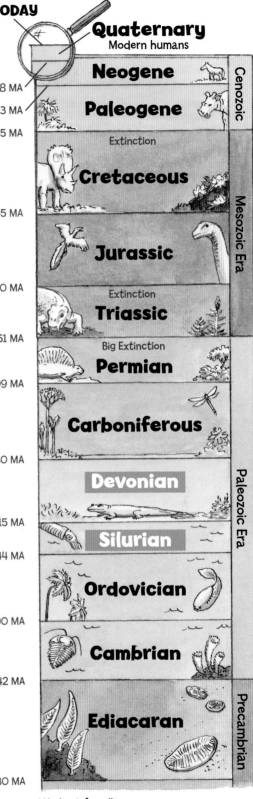

This time line at the right shows the periods of geologic history, going all the way back to when the seas first began to fill with animal life. This section covers the Silurian and the Devonian periods.

MA stands for million years ago.
(In Latin, "million years" is *mega annum*.)

LAND HO!

Why were there so few plants in the Silurian? Why were plants so slow to take advantage of all that empty real estate? The reason is that dry land is a harsh environment for life-forms used to soaking in a bath all day. It's no coincidence that life began in the oceans. Water keeps living things moist, protects them from too much ultraviolet radiation from the sun, and brings food and gases directly to their cellular doorstep.

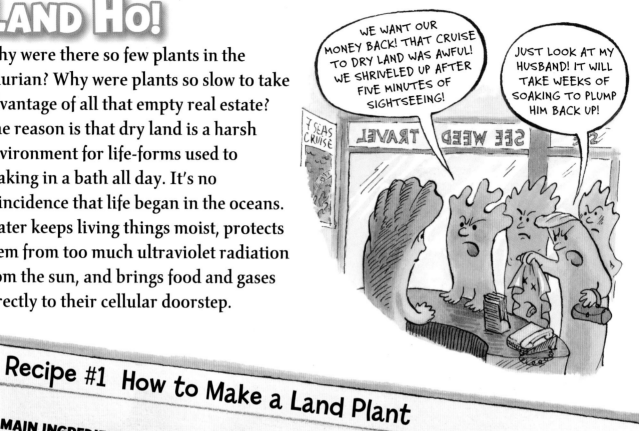

Recipe #1 How to Make a Land Plant

MAIN INGREDIENT: Freshwater green algae

1. Take some freshwater algae and cover it in a waterproof wrapper, called a cuticle, so it won't dry out.

2. Make little holes in the cuticle to let air in and out. Remember, plants need to breathe!

Close-up of cuticle. The holes are called stomata.

3. Put a weatherproof coating on the plant's spores so they can travel through air instead of water. Spores are tiny packets of genetic material for making a new plant. They are smaller and simpler than seeds, which evolved later on.

4. If you want your plant to get bigger, you'll have to put in little pipes so it can suck up water from the ground and bring it to the rest of the plant.

The very first plants had no plumbing. They were related to modern liverworts and mosses.

Plants probably got their start when some freshwater algae figured out how not to become toast every time the pond they lived in dried up. We don't know when this first happened. The oldest fossils of actual bits of plant are from the early Silurian, but scientists have found fossil plant spores that are much older.

Actually, the very first colonizers of land might not have been plants at all, but lichens, which are a partnership between an alga and a fungus. To this day lichens like to make their home on bare rocks, something there were plenty of in the Silurian. Lichens may have paved the way for plants by putting a first thin crust of living matter on the landscape.

Lichens

As soon as there were enough plants, fungi, and other goodies on land to provide some food, animals crawled out of the water to join the fun. The oldest land animal fossils are of arthropods.

Recipe #2 How to Make a Land Animal

MAIN INGREDIENT:
An aquatic arthropod
(an animal with a jointed shell)

1. Strengthen the arthropod's shell and muscles so that the animal can walk around easily on land, where everything weighs much more than in the water.

2. Put a waxy coating on the shell to keep the bug from drying out.

BUG WAX
PROTECTS! ADDS SHINE!

3. Bugs need to breathe, too! Make little holes in the shell to let air into tubes called tracheae, which will take the air to the rest of the animal's body.

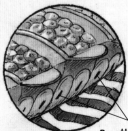

Breathing holes, called spiracles

PNEUMODESMUS. This little millipede is the oldest known land animal. It lived in the middle Silurian. $1\frac{3}{8}$ in (3.5 cm) long

PALAEOTARBUS, a trigonotarbid (an extinct relative of spiders) from the late Silurian, 1/16 in (2 mm) long

Note: This is just one of several possible recipes for making a land animal. You'll need quite a different recipe if you want to make a worm or four-legged animal!

21

GETTING GREENER

Plants kept a low profile in Silurian times, but all sorts of new plants took off in the beginning of the Devonian period. That's where we are now, on a warm, humid day in Quebec, Canada. Nowadays plants fight for space, but 400 million years ago there was still a lot of elbow room, and each plant could send out runners and spread out as much as it liked. The landscape looked like a giant patchwork quilt, with just one species of plant per patch.

Prototaxites

Pertica, at 3 ft (1 m) high, was the tallest plant around.

Sawdonia

Most of these plants were short, but you may have noticed some tall things looming in the distance. Scientists have found log-like fossils called *Prototaxites* up to 30 feet (8 m) long. Trees didn't evolve until later in the Devonian, and parks with obelisks in them were a good 400 million years away, so what could these logs have been? One possibility is that they were mega-mushrooms, giant fungi that towered above the surrounding vegetation.

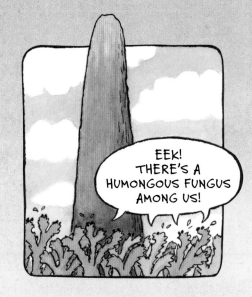

EEK! THERE'S A HUMONGOUS FUNGUS AMONG US!

...and Buggier

Scurrying around under the new plants were a number of new bugs. Centipedes, millipedes, mites, and trigonotarbids had been around since the Silurian. Now they were joined by springtails (six-legged relatives of insects), daddy longlegs, and the oldest known true insect, *Rhyniognatha*.

Eophalangium,
a daddy longlegs

Rhyniella,
a springtail

Rhyniognatha,
the oldest known insect.
Only the head got preserved,
so we have no clue
what the body looked like.

Psilophyton,
a shorter relative of *Pertica*

Prototaxites log

23

THE BIRTH OF DIRT

Once plants had spread out sideways all they could, they began to bump into each other and to fight for light and for a good place to send out their spores. The result? They invented a stiff main trunk and shot upward. They also developed primitive leaves to catch more light.

The plants we see here grew in New York State in the middle of the Devonian. By then there were big shrubs and even trees. Longer roots developed to anchor these larger plants and to collect enough water and minerals for them. Deeper roots and more plant matter meant that a significant amount of dirt—more correctly, soil—began to build up for the first time.

Lepidosigillaria

Wattieza is the earliest known tree. It was over 34 ft (8 m) tall. There is a whole forest of fossil *Wattieza* trunks in Gilboa, New York.

Tetraxylopteris, an extinct relative of modern woody plants

Leclercqia

Leclercqia and *Lepidosigillaria* belonged to a group of plants called lycopods. Only a few small lycopods survive today.

We take soil for granted, but it barely existed before plants became common. Acids in plants help break bits of rock into smaller and smaller pieces, and these mix with organic matter (dead plants and the fungi, bacteria, and animals that help them fall apart) to form soil. Soil in turn supports more happy plants, which help create more soil, and so on toward an ever greener planet.

NO DIRT? HOW DID THEY MANAGE?

Bigger, Better Bugs

Bugs in the meantime had also gotten bigger and more varied. Spiders and centipedes crawled around under the new, improved plants searching for fellow bugs to eat. The rest of the bugs all ate rotting plant matter. Most bugs still hadn't figured out how to eat fresh plants, which are hard to digest. Instead they had to wait for bacteria and fungi in the soil to have a go at the plants first. Among these eaters of leftovers were millipedes, mites, worms (we assume—as usual, they didn't fossilize), and springtails.

ROTTEN SALAD BAR

SPORE TOPPING

FUNGUS DRESSING

Freshwater habitats had more life in them, thanks to nutrients from all the plants on the land around them.

THE DEVONIAN PLANET

The Devonian period got its name from Devonshire, in the south of England, where rocks and fossils from this period were first studied. The Devonian, which began around 415 million years ago, lasted for 55 million years. That's twice as long as the Silurian.

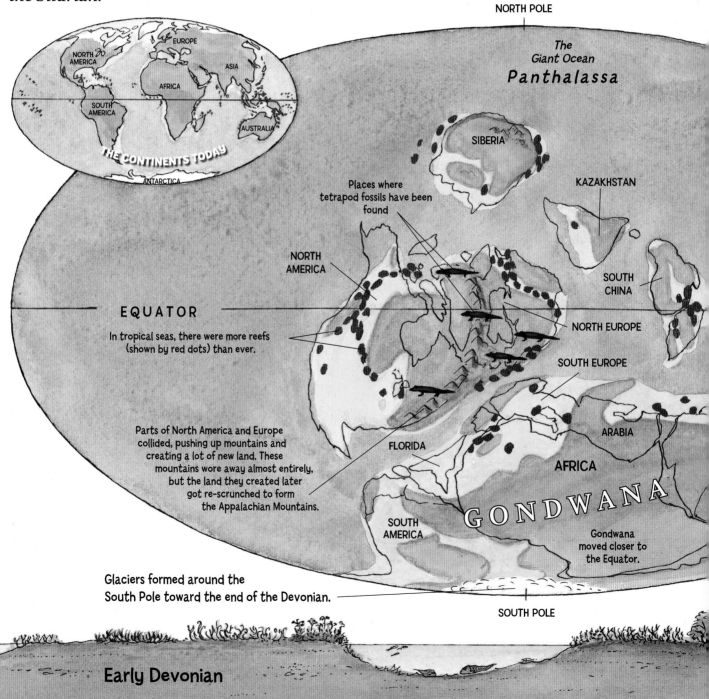

THE CONTINENTS TODAY

NORTH AMERICA · EUROPE · ASIA · AFRICA · SOUTH AMERICA · AUSTRALIA · ANTARCTICA

NORTH POLE

The Giant Ocean **Panthalassa**

SIBERIA

KAZAKHSTAN

Places where tetrapod fossils have been found

NORTH AMERICA

SOUTH CHINA

EQUATOR

NORTH EUROPE

In tropical seas, there were more reefs (shown by red dots) than ever.

SOUTH EUROPE

ARABIA

Parts of North America and Europe collided, pushing up mountains and creating a lot of new land. These mountains wore away almost entirely, but the land they created later got re-scrunched to form the Appalachian Mountains.

FLORIDA

AFRICA

GONDWANA

SOUTH AMERICA

Gondwana moved closer to the Equator.

Glaciers formed around the South Pole toward the end of the Devonian.

SOUTH POLE

Early Devonian

A lot happened in the Devonian. Fish became major players for the first time. They became so common and diverse in both fresh and salt water that the Devonian is sometimes referred to as the Age of Fishes.

On land, a green revolution took place that changed the planet forever. The vegetation went from ankle-high plants to full-fledged forests inhabited by all sorts of bugs ... and us! OK, not us exactly, but our distant ancestors, the first tetrapods, or four-legged animals.

AFTER MANY MILLIONS OF YEARS OF WARM WEATHER, WE'RE IN FOR A COLD SNAP, SO PLEASE BUNDLE UP!

NORTH CHINA

Australia, famous nowadays for its Great Barrier Reef, had equally impressive reefs 375 million years ago, and the waters beyond the reefs were teeming with fish.

AUSTRALIA

ANTARCTICA

As the Devonian came to a close, a series of extinctions hit warm-water marine life especially hard. The culprit? Some scientists think it was plants! Plants back then may have taken in so much carbon dioxide—the greenhouse gas that keeps our planet warm—that they caused a spell of global cooling. (Nowadays we have too much carbon dioxide in the air, and it is causing global warming.) It seems that the cold temperatures were one of the reasons that many warm-water creatures died off, including most of the lovely reef-builders. It took a long time for reefs to recover.

Middle Devonian

Late Devonian

FISHY NEWS

The big news in the fish world had to do with jaws. Fish came up with jaws in the late Ordovician, although jaws didn't become common until much later, in the Devonian. All sorts of new fish evolved as a result. Jaws turned out to be a most versatile tool. They allowed fish to say good-bye to a monotonous diet of teensy stuff. Now fish could grab, slice, and dice to their heart's content. They could even eat one another, and they did so with great gusto. In many environments, fish became top predators, usurping this honor from the eurypterids. Vertebrates—fish and their four-legged descendants—have kept the title of top predator ever since, both in the water and on land.

The Devonian Herald

October 20, 405 MA

"JAWS" TAKE OVER
ORDOVICIAN INVENTION CATCHES ON BIG TIME IN THE DEVONIAN

Dr. Akanth of the University of Southern Gondwana gave us a demonstration last night of how the new body part works. It consists of two sections, an upper and a lower jaw. Each jaw is normally lined with rows of hard pointy things called teeth. Dr. Akanth, who has jaws herself, cannot say enough good things about them. "My biggest fear is that I'll become fat because I can eat so many more things than I could before," she said. Dr. Akanth predicts that it won't be long before most fish have jaws.

LOCAL NEWS – Three Teenage Placoderms Rescued from Drying Pond

The three East Gondwana residents had
e small pond when the
el feet.

THE GREAT DEVONIAN FISH RACE

At the beginning of the Devonian, four groups of fish with jaws—acanthodians, placoderms, sharks, and bony fish—took off in a race to see who would become most common and diverse. Jawless fish were still around, mucking around on the bottom beneath their jawed cousins, but they became less and less common. By the end of the Devonian they had petered out almost entirely.

GET READY, GET SET...

① ACANTHODIANS

Acanthodians were distinguished by having a spine in front of each fin—a prickly mouthful for anyone trying to eat them, for sure. The acanthodians got off to an early start; their fossilized fin spines go as far back as the Ordovician period. In fact, they may have been the first fish with jaws. They kept a steady face through the Devonian and beyond, only to finally go extinct in the Permian.

Climatius, from Britain, 5.5 in (14 cm) long

Parexus, a super-spiny acanthodian, also from Britain; a little over 6 in (16 cm) long

Howittacanthus lived in Australia. It swam with its mouth open to filter plankton, much the way modern-day anchovies do. 10 in (25 cm) long

The placoderms were the group of fish that grew the fastest at the beginning of the Devonian, with many new species cropping up. Placoderms had an armored head and trunk, often with a hinge between the two parts that allowed the mouth to open wider.

Placoderms were generally on the small side, but they did produce some giants such as *Dunkleosteus*, the terror of late Devonian seas. *Dunkleosteus* could be up to 20 feet (6 m) long. It had big, razor-sharp ridges of bone instead of individual teeth.

Dunkleosteus is seen chasing a small shark. 20 ft (6 m) long

The most common placoderm of all was the bug-eyed *Bothriolepis.* This fish had crablike front fins and eyes that stuck up out of holes in the head armor.

Were you hoping to buy a placoderm for your aquarium? Sorry! After being top fish for millions of years, placoderms faded out at the end of the Devonian, never to be seen again.

Bothriolepis, about 1 ft (30 cm) long

The first sharks appeared as far back as the Ordovician, but we don't know what they looked like because all they left behind were microscopic pointy scales. Could the earliest sharks have been toothless? We don't know! The first fossil shark teeth are from the early Devonian. Like sharks today, Devonian sharks replaced old teeth with new ones throughout their lifetime. Devonian sharks did so fairly slowly, but later sharks shed teeth with such abandon that shark teeth became the most common vertebrate fossils in the world.

Cladoselache lived in North America in the late Devonian. About 4 ft (1.2 m) long

A small bony fish is about to become *Cladoselache's* lunch. *Cladoselache* in turn probably had to avoid becoming lunch for giant placoderms such as *Dunkleosteus*.

The mouth of early sharks was at the front of the head. In modern sharks it is below.

Fossils of whole sharks, on the other hand, are extremely rare. Sharks and their relatives are known as cartilaginous fish because their skeleton is made entirely of cartilage rather than bone. Cartilage is softer than bone and usually falls apart before it can fossilize.

Assorted Devonian shark teeth. Scientists can tell prehistoric sharks apart by their teeth.

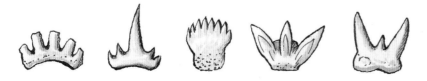

AS WE APPROACH THE FINISH LINE, THE SHARKS ARE KEEPING A STEADY PACE, BUT THE PLACODERMS ARE LOSING STEAM!

Bony fish account for 96 percent of all fish alive today, from minnows to tuna, electric eels, and colorful coral reef fish. Their humble beginnings consist of a few scales and teeth from the Silurian, but like the other contestants in this race, bony fish really got going in the Devonian. Some special features of bony fish are a skeleton made of true bone (as opposed to cartilage, as in sharks), overlapping scales, and, surprisingly, a lung in addition to their gills. In most bony fish alive today, the lung has turned into a swim bladder. This is a bag of gas that keeps the fish from sinking.

Early in the Devonian, the bony fish split into two big groups, the ray-fins and the lobe-fins. They are distinguished by—surprise, surprise!—the structure of their fins.

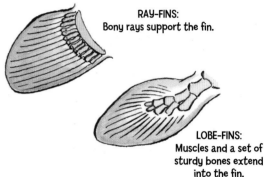

RAY-FINS:
Bony rays support the fin.

LOBE-FINS:
Muscles and a set of sturdy bones extend into the fin.

Mimia, a common little ray-fin from Australia, up to 8 in (20 cm) long

Ray-fins

These are what we think of as "regular fish." The vast majority of living fish are ray-fins, but in the Devonian their numbers were more modest.

These fish all lived in eastern Canada in the late Devonian.

Cheirolepis, a ray-fin fish, up to 20 in (50 cm) long

Eusthenopteron, a large lobe-fin predator, up to 3 ft (1 m) long

Lobe-fins

Lobe-fins did very well in the Devonian, better even than their ray-fin relatives. Many of the larger lobe-fins became top predators, especially in freshwater environments. Nowadays the only surviving lobe-fins are three kinds of lungfishes and a single kind of coelacanth (pronounced SEE-luh-canth), a fish that was thought to have become extinct along with the dinosaurs but which turned up alive in the 1930s in the Indian Ocean. These surviving lobe-fins are our closest living fish relatives.

The Winners

Our direct ancestors, though, were neither lungfishes nor coelacanths. We descend from another branch on the lobe-fin family tree, one that gave rise to all four-legged animals, or tetrapods. Although the fishes in this group eventually became extinct, their descendants are alive and well in the form of every single amphibian, reptile, bird, and mammal on the planet. Throw in the ray-fins as well, and we see that Devonian bony fish are the ancestors of all living vertebrates except for sharks and their kin, lampreys, and hagfishes. Bony fish are clearly the winners of the race!

BONY FISH HAVE WON THE GOLD! SHARKS ARE IN SECOND PLACE.

FIRST PLACE

SECOND PLACE

Elpistostege, a very close relative of tetrapods, up to 5 ft (1.5 m)

Miguashaia, an oddly shaped coelacanth, up to 18 in (45 cm) long

Scaumenacia, a lungfish, up to 24 in (60 cm) long

THE FIRST FORESTS

Meanwhile, back on land, a tree called *Archaeopteris* (not to be confused with the Jurassic bird *Archaeopteryx*) created the world's first real forests. *Archaeopteris* had deep roots and a solid wood trunk very much like that of a pine tree. Its leaves, on the other hand, looked fernlike. And like a fern, *Archaeopteris* reproduced by means of spores—a strange hodgepodge indeed! Hodgepodge or not, it was wildly successful for much of the late Devonian. It grew from the tropics all the way to fairly cool regions. Like all spore plants, it always stuck fairly close to water, since spore plants need moisture in order to reproduce.

Archaeopteris won the fight for light, hands down. Not only was it taller than the competition, it also had improved leaves that created a denser shade.

Archaeopteris

TRY GROWING THROUGH THAT, SUCKER!

And in case that wasn't enough, it shed its branches from time to time, smothering whatever was trying to sprout below it. Forest soils became especially thick and moist thanks to the shade, the leaf litter, and the longer roots holding everything in place.

Seeds of Change

After being so successful, *Archaeopteris* dwindled and finally disappeared right near the end of the Devonian. Nobody knows why. The future, in any case, belonged to the new kids on the block: plants that made seeds. All the plants we have seen so far were spore plants, like our living ferns and mosses. In the Devonian, some plants gradually went from making spores to making seeds. These new seed plants were able to grow in all sorts of different environments, including places that were too harsh or dry for spore plants.

Rhacophyton, a fern relative

Elkinsia, one of the first seed plants

LITTERBUGS

Shady Devonian forests with lots of leaf litter were bug heavens. Many of the bugs back then were similar to bugs we have in our forests today. Among the predators were scorpions, spiders, and centipedes, all happily munching the rest of the bugs, namely millipedes, springtails, mites, insects, and more. The vegetarian bugs continued to feed mostly on nature's garbage—rotting plant matter and fungi—but some bugs apparently pierced plant stems to lap the juices. Others may have eaten spores or pollen.

Flying insects don't appear as fossils until the Carboniferous period. It is likely that they already existed in the late Devonian, though we can't know for sure.

Flying insects? We can only guess what they might have looked like.

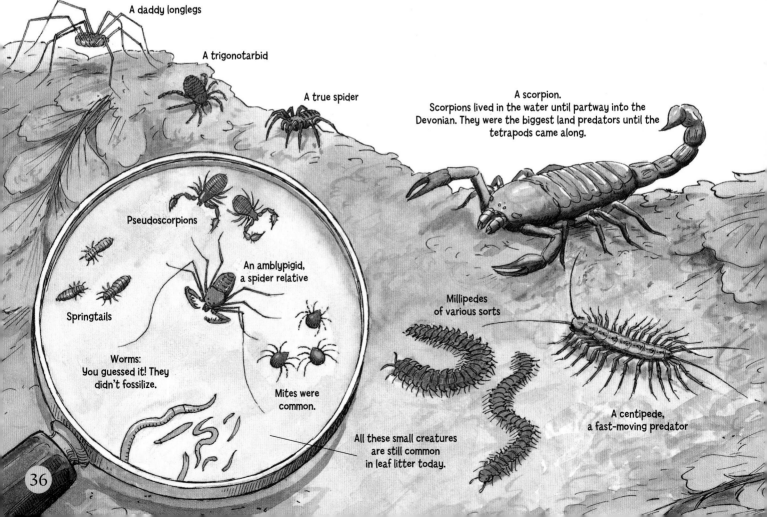

A daddy longlegs

A trigonotarbid

A true spider

A scorpion.
Scorpions lived in the water until partway into the Devonian. They were the biggest land predators until the tetrapods came along.

Pseudoscorpions

An amblypigid, a spider relative

Springtails

Worms:
You guessed it! They didn't fossilize.

Mites were common.

Millipedes of various sorts

A centipede, a fast-moving predator

All these small creatures are still common in leaf litter today.

LAND HO ... AGAIN!

In the shallow streams and lakes of the late Devonian, some lobe-fin fishes were experimenting with becoming four-legged and leaving the water. A fish that could crawl and breathe air could live in waters that were too shallow for other predators. It could also walk overland to ponds that other fish couldn't reach. Who knows, it might even pick up a few crunchy, high-protein snacks along the way, namely bugs.

What changes did fish have to make in order to become land animals? They had to be able to breathe air, of course, but this was relatively simple. As we have seen, bony fish had already invented lungs as a way to survive in oxygen-poor waters. All tetrapods had to do was perfect these lungs and add better mechanisms for pumping air into them. The trickier and more innovative part of becoming a land animal had to do with changes in the skeleton, as we shall see on the next page.

Tiktaalik, a 375-million-year-old fish from northern Canada, had the scales and fins of a fish, but it had leg-like bones in its fins and could use them to shuffle onto land. Scientists jokingly call it a "fishapod."

HOW WE GOT FEET

Here are four creatures that illustrate how the skeleton changed as fish evolved into four-legged animals. They are all from the late Devonian—except for the dachshund, of course!

Arms and Legs

The sturdy bones in the fins of lobe-fins are a sneak preview of the bones in our own arms and legs. This made lobe-fins the perfect candidates for becoming four-legged. *Tiktaalik* could even crawl along on its fins.

Fingers and Toes

Fingers and toes came next. Whether squeezing by plants in vegetation-choked waters or crawling onto land, a sturdy paddle with fingers in it was more useful than a delicate fish fin.

The Neck

Can you imagine us without a neck? We would all look like Humpty Dumpty. If you look at *Eusthenopteron*, you will see that the shoulder bones are stuck to the head. In *Tiktaalik* and in tetrapods there is a space between the head and the shoulder bones, allowing the head to move freely.

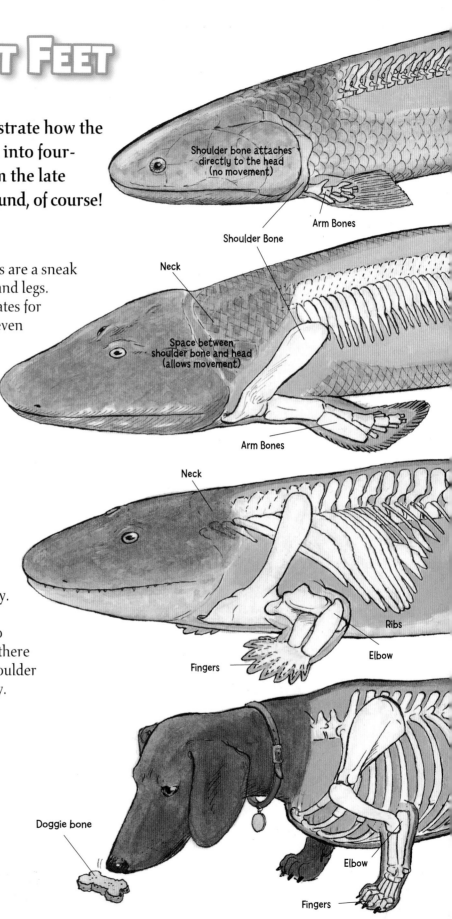

Shoulder bone attaches directly to the head (no movement)

Arm Bones

Shoulder Bone

Neck

Space between shoulder bone and head (allows movement)

Arm Bones

Neck

Ribs

Elbow

Fingers

Doggie bone

Elbow

Fingers

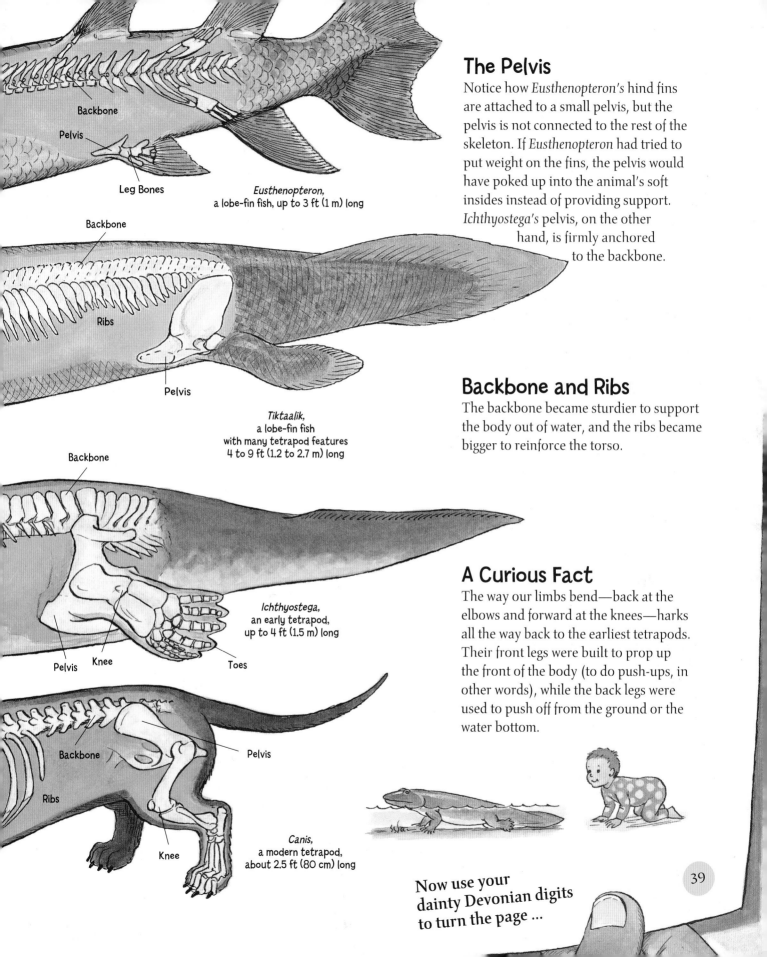

Backbone

Pelvis

Leg Bones

Eusthenopteron,
a lobe-fin fish, up to 3 ft (1 m) long

The Pelvis

Notice how *Eusthenopteron's* hind fins are attached to a small pelvis, but the pelvis is not connected to the rest of the skeleton. If *Eusthenopteron* had tried to put weight on the fins, the pelvis would have poked up into the animal's soft insides instead of providing support. *Ichthyostega's* pelvis, on the other hand, is firmly anchored to the backbone.

Backbone

Ribs

Pelvis

Tiktaalik,
a lobe-fin fish
with many tetrapod features
4 to 9 ft (1.2 to 2.7 m) long

Backbone and Ribs

The backbone became sturdier to support the body out of water, and the ribs became bigger to reinforce the torso.

Backbone

Ichthyostega,
an early tetrapod,
up to 4 ft (1.5 m) long

Pelvis   Knee   Toes

A Curious Fact

The way our limbs bend—back at the elbows and forward at the knees—harks all the way back to the earliest tetrapods. Their front legs were built to prop up the front of the body (to do push-ups, in other words), while the back legs were used to push off from the ground or the water bottom.

Backbone   Pelvis

Ribs

Knee

Canis,
a modern tetrapod,
about 2.5 ft (80 cm) long

Now use your
dainty Devonian digits
to turn the page ...

STEPPING INTO
THE FUTURE

Here we are on a warm, cloudy day near the end of the Devonian, in what is now Greenland. Two *Ichthyostega* are lumbering around on a riverbank. *Ichthyostega* was slow and clumsy on land, but its fellow tetrapods were no better, so who cared?

Scientists have discovered about a dozen different Devonian tetrapods so far. These animals were amphibians. They laid their eggs in the water and probably spent most of their adult life in the water as well.

We don't know exactly which early tetrapod was our direct ancestor. We do know, however, that we descend from some relative of *Ichthyostega*, which in the next period, the Carboniferous, abandoned its amphibious lifestyle and gave rise to the ancestors of both reptiles and mammals. Stay tuned! Our slippery, jelly-egged ancestors will return in *Part II: When Bugs Were Big.*

The Shoe Industry Honors **ICHTHYOSTEGA** One of the Inventors of FEET

AS I ACCEPT THIS PRESTIGIOUS AWARD, I WOULD LIKE TO THANK EVERYONE WHO MADE LIFE ON LAND POSSIBLE IN THE FIRST PLACE: THANK YOU MICROBES, ALGAE, FUNGI, PLANTS, AND BUGS! WE WOULDN'T BE HERE IF IT WEREN'T FOR YOU!

Part 11

WHEN BUGS WERE BIG, PLANTS WERE STRANGE, & TETRAPODS STALKED THE EARTH

A Cartoon Prehistory of Life Before Dinosaurs

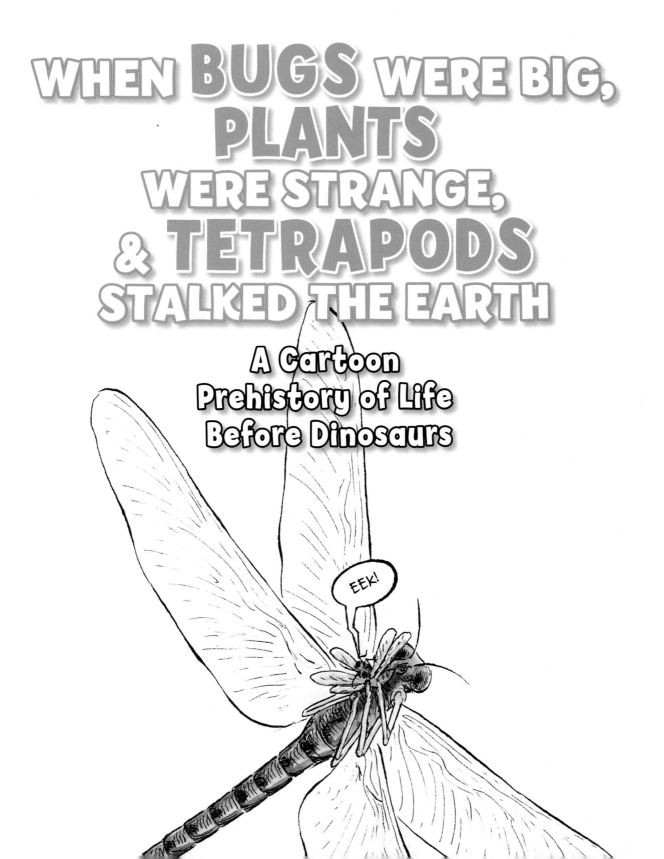

EEK!

Welcome to the COAL SWAMPS

Mid-afternoon, 320 million years ago. It rained this morning, but now the sun is out and steam is rising from the coal swamps. Rivers meander out toward the sea through huge marshy deltas that are covered in strange forests.

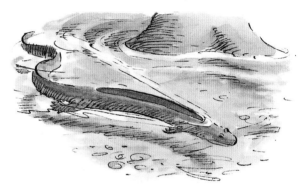

It's very quiet except for some buzzing insects and the sound of water rippling as an amphibian swims by.

TODAY WILL BE HOT AND MUGGY, JUST LIKE EVERY OTHER DAY FOR THE NEXT SEVERAL MILLION YEARS! SHOWERS LIKELY.

80°
92°
93°
86°

Let's take a look at the plants that grew in the swamps back then. The tall trees belong to an ancient group called lycopods. The young ones looked like hairy telephone poles, the full-grown ones like something out of a Dr. Seuss book.

The only lycopods still alive today are club mosses and their relatives, puny little plants you might find on the forest floor. Ancient lycopod trees came in a variety of shapes. Scientists have given them long Latin names.

Diaphorodendron   *Paralycopodites*   *Sigillaria*

One of the strangest things about these trees was how they grew. First the baby tree put out roots. The roots had little rootlets that could come up above the mud and photosynthesize, which means they could make their own food from sunlight. The bark on the trunks may also have been green and photosynthetic.

In a mere ten years the tree could be 90 feet (27 m) tall. Only then did it put out branches, in order to have someplace from which to dangle its cones. The cones released spores, which the wind carried away.

Spore cone

Spores

Lepidodendron

Where leaves fell off, they left a pretty diamond-shape pattern.

Seven-foot (2-m) basketball player for scale

47

Other plants were more familiar looking. Some of the ferns would have looked just fine in a pot in someone's living room—a waste of talent, since living rooms hadn't been invented yet. Others were tree size.

Horsetails, ferns, and lycopods all grow from spores. A spore is a tiny packet of genetic material that needs to be wet in order to turn into a new plant. The rainy, soggy swamps were a paradise for spore plants.

A tree fern. There are similar-looking tree ferns alive today in places such as New Guinea.

A seed fern—not really a fern at all but an early seed plant

Cordaites, another early seed plant

Primitive horsetails. Similar ones still grow in damp places nowadays. Some of the early ones formed big bushes and even trees.

Fossil Sunshine

What happened to all those megatons of luxuriant, fast-growing plants when they died?

Trees flattened by a storm

Cutting peat

In the swamps the plant matter piled up in the water and became a brown mush called peat. Peat still forms today in places called peat bogs.

Over time, the peat got buried under layers of mud and sand. The peat turned into coal, and the mud and sand turned into rock.

Coal seam

rock

This means that if your local power plant burns coal, then the electricity in your home is really solar energy captured by plants hundreds of millions of years ago through photosynthesis.

WE ... AHEM!
ATTENTION PLEASE, CLASS! WE CALL THIS PERIOD THE CARBONIFEROUS BECAUSE OF ALL THE COAL IT PRODUCED.

CARBO = LATIN FOR COAL

CARBONIFEROUS PERIOD
360 - 299 MILLION YEARS AGO

THE CARBONIFEROUS PLANET

How come we find remains of tropical coal swamps in places such as Canada and Germany, which are now quite chilly? Well, during the Carboniferous period those places weren't chilly at all, and that's because of something called continental drift. Ever since they first formed, the continents have been doing the world's slowest dance, sliding around on sections of the Earth's crust called plates. Back in Carboniferous times, the continents were farther south than they are now. North America and Europe were on the Equator, where it is hottest.

IT'S NICE AND TOASTY NEAR THE EQUATOR, BUT IF YOU'RE TRAVELING SOUTH, YOU'D BETTER BRING A SCARF ALONG!

85° 87° 90° 80° 40°

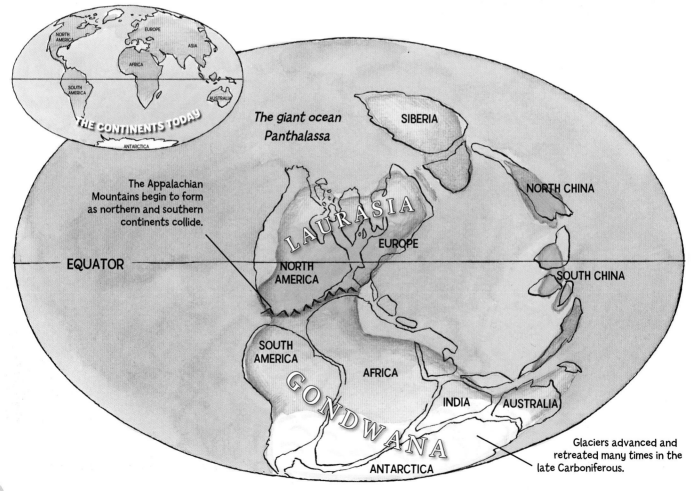

THE CONTINENTS TODAY

NORTH AMERICA
EUROPE
ASIA
AFRICA
SOUTH AMERICA
AUSTRALIA
ANTARCTICA

The giant ocean Panthalassa

SIBERIA

NORTH CHINA

The Appalachian Mountains begin to form as northern and southern continents collide.

LAURASIA

EUROPE

EQUATOR

NORTH AMERICA

SOUTH CHINA

SOUTH AMERICA

AFRICA

GONDWANA

INDIA   AUSTRALIA

ANTARCTICA

Glaciers advanced and retreated many times in the late Carboniferous.

CRUNCH!

These plates apparently have no sense of direction because they keep bumping into each other. When this happens, the land gets scrunched, and mountain ranges rise up. During the Carboniferous, the southern continent of Gondwana collided with North America and Europe and created mountains that include the Appalachians.

During the second half, the Poles froze over every hundred thousand years or so. When they did, lots of water got locked up as ice and sea levels went down. This exposed big flat areas of coastline in the rainy tropics that were perfect places for coal swamps to grow.

Then the ice would melt and sea levels would go up again, and sand and mud covered the swamps. This happened over and over, creating the layers of coal and rock that we just saw on page 49.

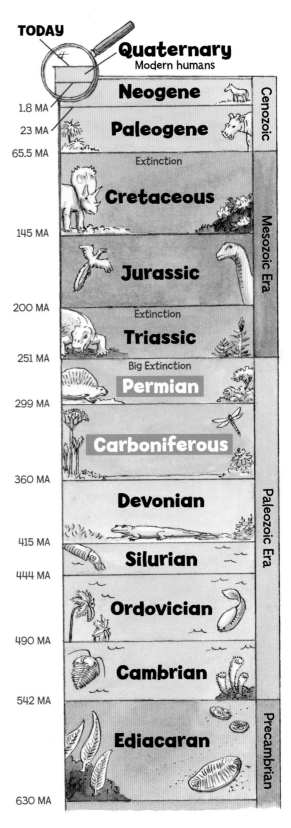

TODAY

Quaternary
Modern humans

Neogene — Cenozoic
1.8 MA
Paleogene
23 MA
65.5 MA

Extinction
Cretaceous — Mesozoic Era
145 MA

Jurassic
200 MA

Extinction
Triassic
251 MA

Big Extinction
Permian
299 MA

Carboniferous — Paleozoic Era
360 MA

Devonian
415 MA
Silurian
444 MA
Ordovician
490 MA
Cambrian
542 MA

Ediacaran — Precambrian
630 MA

MA stands for million years ago.
(In Latin, "million years" is *mega annum*.)

BIG BUG, LITTLE BUG

Now let's get back to the swamp! Until this time, the only things crisscrossing the air had been leaves, dust, and spores carried by the wind. Now for the first time there were insects buzzing around in the humid air overhead. With bats and birds and flying reptiles still many millions of years away, these aerial pioneers could flit about at their leisure … unless a dragonfly the size of a small falcon came cruising along with an appetite!

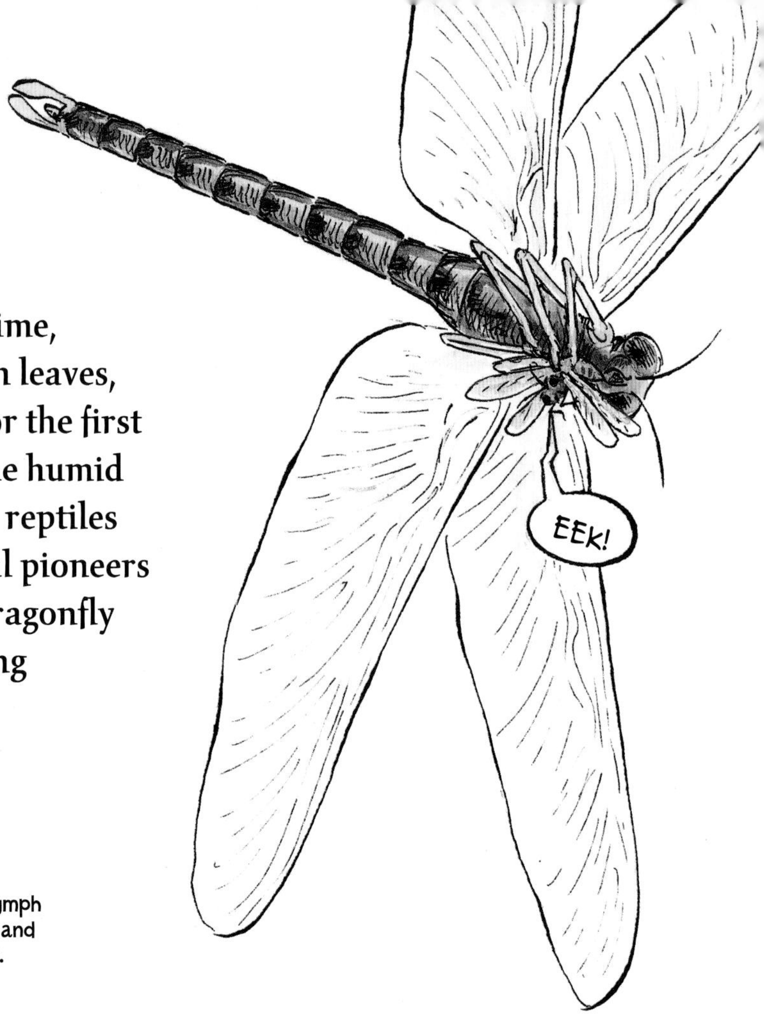

EEk!

The dragonfly's carnivorous nymph must have been equally huge and the terror of local swamps.

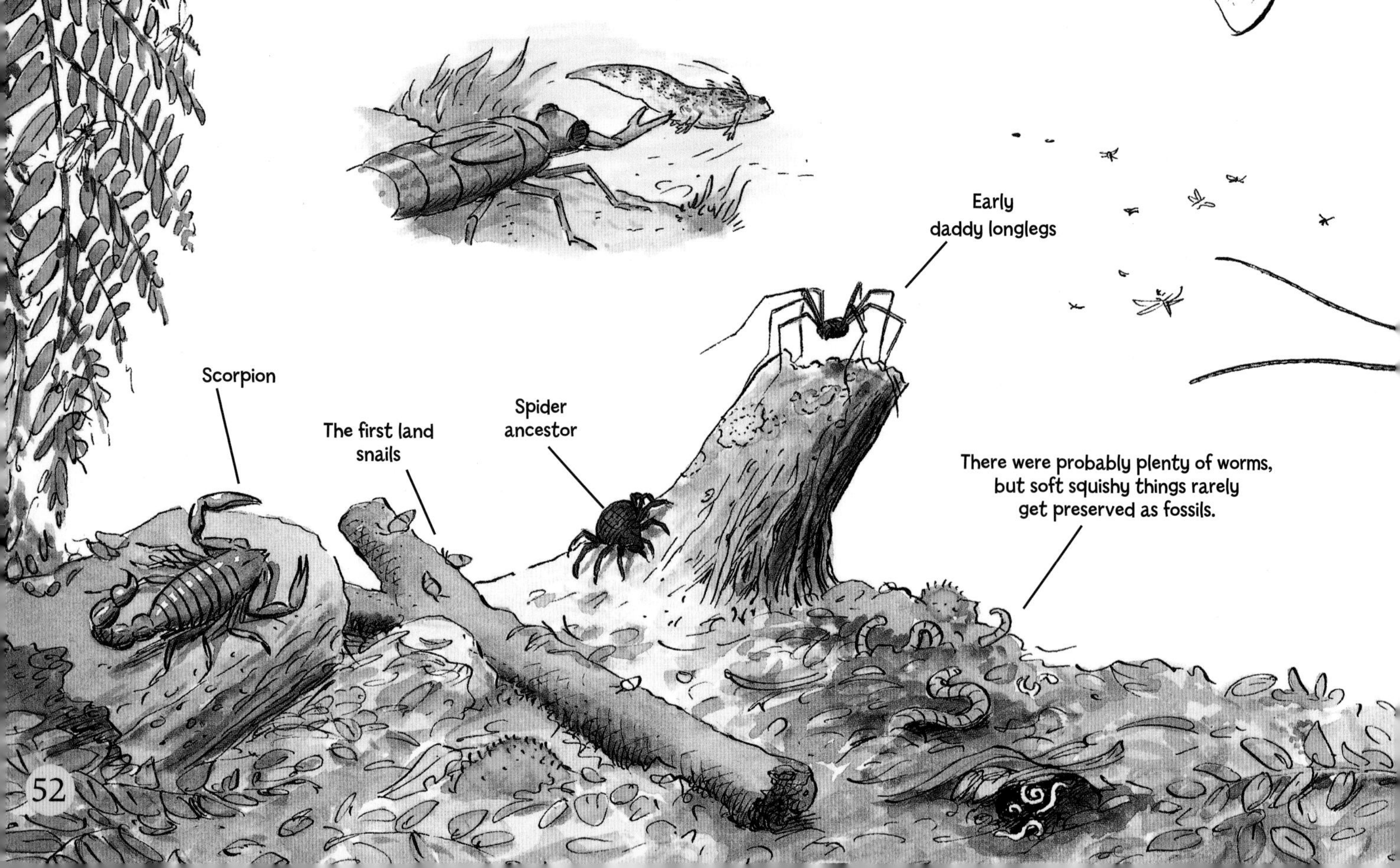

Scorpion

The first land snails

Spider ancestor

Early daddy longlegs

There were probably plenty of worms, but soft squishy things rarely get preserved as fossils.

The most common insects around were the ancestors of cockroaches. The leaf litter was teeming with them. Nowadays they seem especially fond of kitchens, as anyone who's gone for a midnight snack in certain New York City apartments will tell you. What makes roaches so successful that they're still all over the place today? It's probably that they're not picky eaters (they'll eat anything from rotting Carboniferous plants to wallpaper, soap, or moldy Cheerios); they like to live in warm places; and they reproduce very, very fast.

The vast majority of these insects were no bigger than their modern relatives, but many insect groups did produce at least a few XXL models. The biggest were the dragonflies, followed by mayflies and the extinct palaeodictyopterans, some of which had a 16-inch (40-cm) wingspan—the same as a robin's.

OHIO, 300 MILLION YEARS AGO

MANHATTAN, ZERO YEARS AGO

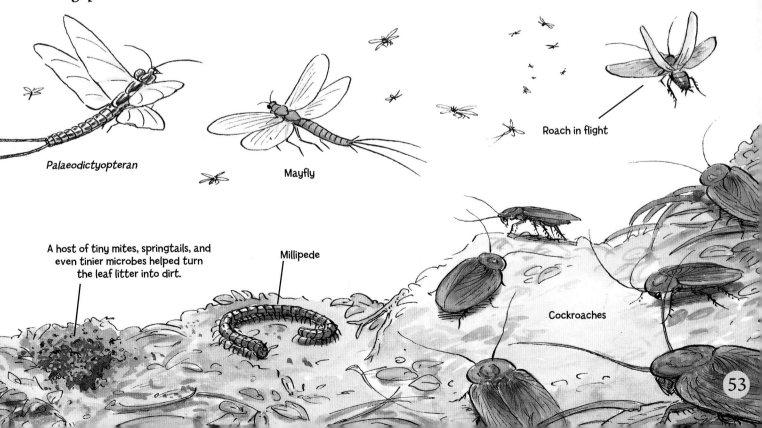

Palaeodictyopteran

Mayfly

Roach in flight

A host of tiny mites, springtails, and even tinier microbes helped turn the leaf litter into dirt.

Millipede

Cockroaches

The biggest bug of all was not an insect. Imagine for a moment that you're sitting under a tree fern minding your own business, when you hear rustling noises worthy of a freight train, and along comes a 6-foot (1.8-m)-long thing that looks like a huge, flattened centipede. It's called *Arthropleura*. Luckily for you, it's a harmless vegetarian that uses its immensely long gut to digest leaf litter with the help of microbes, much the way cows digest hay today.

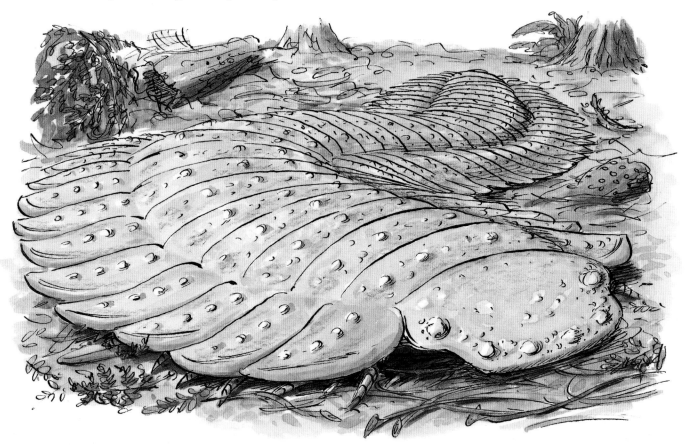

It's a pity we no longer have bugs this big … or perhaps it isn't such a pity, come to think of it! Scientists have wondered why bugs got this big only during this time. One possible explanation has to do with oxygen. There were so many plants growing then that oxygen levels in the air reached an all-time high. A bug doesn't have sophisticated lungs like ours to help it breathe, and if its body is very big it has trouble getting enough oxygen to all its different parts. The high oxygen levels allowed bigger bodies to evolve. Still, bugs didn't get big just because they could; being bigger must have had advantages, such as having fewer enemies, or in this case, being able to digest more food thanks to an extra-long gut.

Winners of the
Big Bug Competition

First Prize:
Arthropleura
6 ft (1.8 m) long.
North America, Europe,
Kazakhstan

Second Prize:
Meganeuropsis permiana
The biggest flying insect ever
Wingspan: 28 in (72 cm).
North America

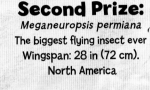

Third Prize:
Pulmonoscorpius
A scorpion
2.5 ft (70 cm) long.
Scotland

**Honorable
Mention:**
Megarachne
A eurypterid
formerly thought to
be a giant spider.
See page 121.
20 in (50 cm) long.
Argentina

Young *Homo sapiens*
(for size comparison)
56 in (1.4 m) long. Worldwide.

**Vaguely buglike
special mention:**
Hibbertopterus
A 6-foot (1.8-m)-long
eurypterid (a relative of
scorpions) that crawled around
in the swamp waters. Scotland

SHARKS and SEASHELLS by the SEASHORE

Orthacanthus could grow up to 10 feet (3 m) long.

The trout-size *Janassa*

The goldfish-size *Xenacanthus*

Underwater, fish continued to evolve. The placoderms that terrorized Devonian waters had gone extinct, whereas sharks were so common that the Carboniferous is sometimes called "The Age of Sharks." One of the weirdest was the three-foot (1-m)-long *Akmonistion*, which sported a mysterious "headdress" covered in spines.

Akmonistion

I THINK THE SHARK HID IN THE SAND, AND THE CREST SCARED OFF PREDATORS.

Scientist

I THINK IT WAS FOR MATING.

Scientist

AND I SAY TOO BAD IT'S EXTINCT 'CAUSE IT WOULD HAVE MADE A TERRIFIC CHEESE GRATER!

Chef

NOBODY KNOWS FOR SURE WHAT AKMONISTION USED ITS SPINY TURRET FOR.

The shallow seas beyond the coal swamps in what is now Illinois were home to jellyfish, shrimplike crustaceans, clams, fish and one of the strangest animals of the entire Carboniferous: the invertebrate *Tullimonstrum gregarium*, known to its human fans as the Tully Monster. As monsters go, it was puny, ranging from 3 to 14 inches (8–35 cm) long. It had a squid-like body, eyes on handlebars, and a long trunk with pincers at the end, a combination so odd that scientists are not sure where to place it on the tree of life.

Bandringa, a long-nosed shark

Belotelson, a shrimp

Tullimonstrum

TOWERING TETRAPODS

Bugs weren't the only oversize inhabitants of the late Paleozoic. Nowadays amphibians are generally small, but prehistoric ones came in all shapes and sizes. Some were big, some were little, some were built to live on land, and some were swimmers. Some even lost their legs and looked like snakes.

Amphibians descended from fish in the Devonian period, and until reptiles appeared in the middle of the Carboniferous, they were the only tetrapods (four-legged creatures) around.

Modern frog for size comparison

Eryops, a big bruiser that spent much of its time in the water. 6.5 ft (2 m)

MOST AMPHIBIANS ATE BUGS.

SOME ALSO ATE FISH.

AND SOME, LIKE DISCOSAURISCUS, EVEN ATE THEIR OWN RELATIVES.

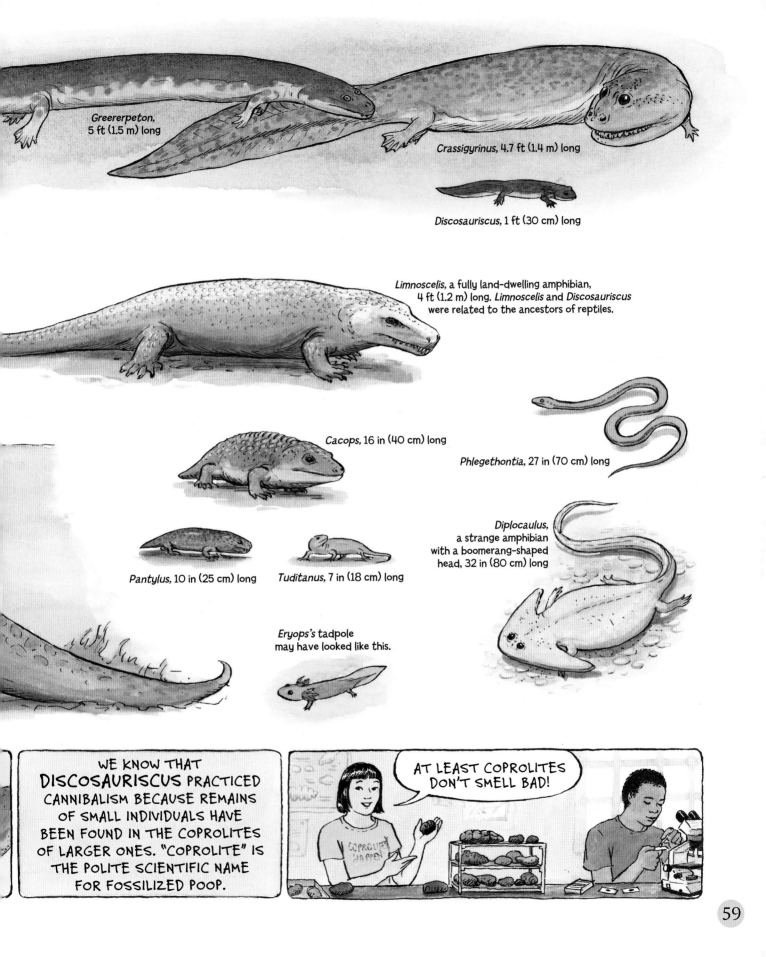

Greererpeton, 5 ft (1.5 m) long

Crassigyrinus, 4.7 ft (1.4 m) long

Discosauriscus, 1 ft (30 cm) long

Limnoscelis, a fully land-dwelling amphibian, 4 ft (1.2 m) long. *Limnoscelis* and *Discosauriscus* were related to the ancestors of reptiles.

Cacops, 16 in (40 cm) long

Phlegethontia, 27 in (70 cm) long

Pantylus, 10 in (25 cm) long

Tuditanus, 7 in (18 cm) long

Diplocaulus, a strange amphibian with a boomerang-shaped head, 32 in (80 cm) long

Eryops's tadpole may have looked like this.

WE KNOW THAT **DISCOSAURISCUS** PRACTICED CANNIBALISM BECAUSE REMAINS OF SMALL INDIVIDUALS HAVE BEEN FOUND IN THE COPROLITES OF LARGER ONES. "COPROLITE" IS THE POLITE SCIENTIFIC NAME FOR FOSSILIZED POOP.

AT LEAST COPROLITES DON'T SMELL BAD!

WHICH CAME FIRST, THE CHICKEN OR THE EGG?

> YOU WOULDN'T BELIEVE WHAT RAISING THESE LITTLE GUYS WITHOUT A POND IS COSTING ME IN ELECTRIC BILLS, EDNA!

AN EARLY ATTEMPT AT INLAND COLONIZATION

Like amphibians today, their prehistoric ancestors all had to lay their eggs in water. The catch: It meant they couldn't live far from a pond. In the meantime, the higher, drier areas were full of tasty bugs—and nobody to eat them. Such a waste! By the middle of the Carboniferous, some tetrapods evolved a type of egg that could be hatched on land. Instead of putting an egg in a pond, they somehow managed to put a pond in an egg: The embryo was now inside a bag of liquid called the amnion. A shell on the outside of the egg prevented it from drying out, and a big yolk fed the embryo so it could skip the tadpole stage and come out of the egg looking like a miniature copy of its parents.

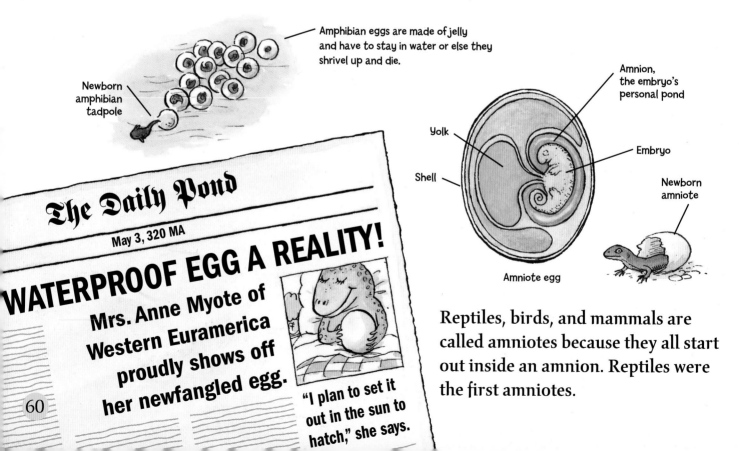

Amphibian eggs are made of jelly and have to stay in water or else they shrivel up and die.

Newborn amphibian tadpole

Amnion, the embryo's personal pond

Yolk

Embryo

Shell

Newborn amniote

Amniote egg

The Daily Pond

May 3, 320 MA

WATERPROOF EGG A REALITY!

Mrs. Anne Myote of Western Euramerica proudly shows off her newfangled egg.

"I plan to set it out in the sun to hatch," she says.

Reptiles, birds, and mammals are called amniotes because they all start out inside an amnion. Reptiles were the first amniotes.

No Paleozoic fossil eggs have been discovered so far. How, then, do paleontologists know which fossils are amniotes and which are not? They have to rely on a number of small differences in the skeleton, and they don't always agree. The oldest amniote ever found is a lizard-like reptile called *Hylonomus*. Fossils of *Hylonomus* were found inside hollow lycopod stumps in Joggins, Nova Scotia (home also to the giant *Arthropleura* and other interesting animals). *Hylonomus* was a small, agile bug catcher. This was a good thing to be in a world with more and more bugs to catch.

Hylonomus, the world's oldest fossil reptile

JOB OPPORTUNITIES

ECOLOGICAL NICHES

Position available for bug eater. Must be willing to travel far from water. Call 627-BUGS.

Bug eaters wanted for unexplored highlands. Plenty of food guaranteed. Sorry, amniotes only. Contact gus@catch.bug.

Start a new life! Seeking colonizers for the hills. Bugs-a-plenty!! No amphibians need apply. Call 800-232-7878.

All the bugs you can eat! Many perks for adventure-some egg-layers. Contact Tim@bugeaters.bug.

ECOLOGICAL NICHES

Full-time position hunti[ng] bugs in dry areas. Send résumé to Reptile Reps[,] PO Box 432, Uplands[.]

Are you a team player[?] Hungry?? Go where n[o] tetrapod has ever gon[e] before!!! E-mail to Bob@bugsorbu[...]

Bug eaters ne[...] untraveled [...] All food, [...] Sorry, ar[...] Contac[...]

Star[...] co[...] E[...] amph[...]

[left column fragments]

ing
eaters
[h]lands.
e time.
[fr]equent.
eat.bug

[...]ion hunting
[...]ands. Call
[...]nd-A-Rep,
[...]1, Hilltown.

Upland Cuisine

Cordaites, a seed plant

NEW FRONTIERS

The earliest amniotes continued to hang out in the lowlands near their amphibian ancestors. Then they gradually began to head for the hills, where they colonized all sorts of new habitats. In the meantime, the climate was changing. In the late Carboniferous, the tropics began to have frequent dry spells and there were glaciers near the South Pole. Most of the lovely, weird lycopod trees went extinct, and seed plants (which first appeared in the Devonian) became much more common. Seed plants were happy in this drier climate because seeds protect the plant embryo from drying out and contain lots of food to give it a good start even if conditions aren't ideal—just as amniote eggs protect and nourish animal embryos.

The Carboniferous was followed by the Permian period. By the early Permian, seed plants had become even more common, and a whole host of amniotes had moved in among them.

Early conifers, ancestors of our pines and firs

Autunia, a seed fern

Sigillaria, the only remaining lycopod tree

Giant horsetails, which still grew in damp places

THE PERMIAN PLANET

The climate continued to get drier in the Permian. By now the continents had all come together into one supercontinent, Pangaea. This changed the pattern of ocean currents and created big inland areas, which tend to have more extreme climates. The continent had also drifted northward, bringing more of the southern landmass out of the freezer and into the temperate zone.

THE PERMIAN WAS NAMED AFTER THE RUSSIAN CITY OF PERM, WHERE THERE ARE SOME EXCELLENT ROCK LAYERS FROM THIS PERIOD.

PERMIAN
299 - 251 MA

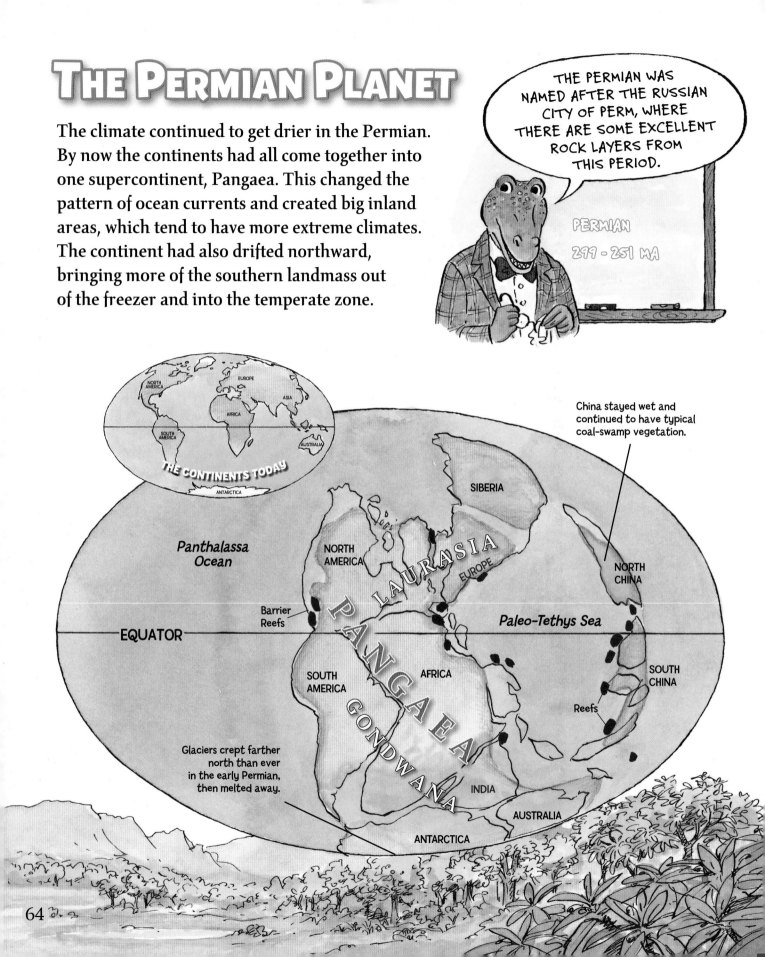

THE CONTINENTS TODAY

NORTH AMERICA
EUROPE
ASIA
AFRICA
SOUTH AMERICA
AUSTRALIA
ANTARCTICA

China stayed wet and continued to have typical coal-swamp vegetation.

SIBERIA

Panthalassa Ocean

NORTH AMERICA

LAURASIA

EUROPE

NORTH CHINA

Barrier Reefs

PANGAEA

Paleo-Tethys Sea

EQUATOR

SOUTH AMERICA

AFRICA

SOUTH CHINA

GONDWANA

Reefs

Glaciers crept farther north than ever in the early Permian, then melted away.

INDIA

AUSTRALIA

ANTARCTICA

Many inland areas became deserts. Entire seas dried up and left behind thick crusts of salt and other minerals. These areas must have looked like the Great Salt Lake in Utah, which is suffering a similar fate.

Meanwhile the wooded parts of the Southern Hemisphere were entirely dominated by a tree called *Glossopteris*. We know that *Glossopteris* had cold winters to contend with because its wood had seasonal rings in it, and because it shed its leaves. *Glossopteris* leaves blanketed the ground every fall just as they do in our temperate forests today.

Bugs continued to be plentiful and many new insect families evolved.

Glossopteris

65

REPTILES ON THE RISE

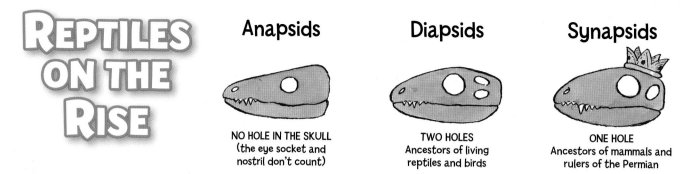

Anapsids

NO HOLE IN THE SKULL
(the eye socket and
nostril don't count)

Diapsids

TWO HOLES
Ancestors of living
reptiles and birds

Synapsids

ONE HOLE
Ancestors of mammals and
rulers of the Permian

Now back to our story! No sooner had reptiles appeared on the scene in the middle of the Carboniferous than they began evolving along three different paths, each with a different kind of skull. Two of the groups developed holes in their skulls that allowed for new and improved jaw muscles.

Anapsids: the No-Holes

Like their amphibian ancestors, the earliest reptiles such as *Hylonomus* had solid anapsid skulls with no holes in them. Later members of the group are a bit of a hodge-podge scientifically speaking, since some of them have little in common apart from the no-hole skull. The anapsids are all extinct … or maybe not! Turtles have no holes in their skulls, but scientists are still trying to figure out whether that's because they're true anapsids, or whether they started out as diapsids and lost their skull holes over time.

Many anapsids were lizard-like, but one group called the pareiasaurs produced some real hulks such as *Scutosaurus*, a Permian plant-eater the size of a small cow.

WOULDN'T YOU LIKE TO BE A SYNAPSID LIKE ME?

ARE YOU KIDDING? I NEED THAT LIKE I NEED A HOLE IN THE HEAD!

Eocaptorhinus, 1 ft (30 cm) long

Scutosaurus,
6.5 ft (2 m) long

Diapsids: Lizards and Dinos and Birds, Oh My!

The diapsids of this period are the ancestors of all living reptiles. They are also the ancestors of dinosaurs, and therefore of birds as well. They started out small and lizard shaped and then branched out into two main groups.

WHAT!— THAT'S MY ANCESTOR?

Petrolacosaurus, the earliest diapsid found so far

The group called the **archosaurs** tended to be large. *Protorosaurus* was a six-foot (1.8-m)-long archosaur that may have eaten bugs or fish. *Archosaurus,* on the other hand, was a fierce meat-eater with a vaguely crocodilian face. This was no coincidence, since the descendants of this group evolved into crocodiles and dinosaurs—but not until the next period, the Triassic.

Archosaurus

Protorosaurus

Members of the other group, the **lepidosauromorphs,** kept their slim and lizardly figures and gave rise to all our modern lizards and snakes.

Hovasaurus, a swimmer

Paliguana

Coelurosauravus, a Permian glider

Meandering Toward Mammalhood: the Synapsids

Forget anapsids and diapsids—the real rulers of the late Carboniferous and of the Permian were the ancestors of mammals, the synapsids. The first wave of them were called pelycosaurs, and they still looked decidedly reptilian. Here we see a group of pelycosaurs called *Edaphosaurus* using the tall sails on their backs as solar panels to catch the first rays of morning sun and get rid of their nighttime chill. Reptiles are sluggish when they're cold, and these plant-eaters are hoping to get up to speed before their carnivorous relative *Dimetrodon* does the same thing.

Dimetrodon had a similar sail. With the sail turned toward the sun, the blood under the surface warmed up quickly. If the animal got too hot, all it had to do was turn the sail away from the sun or stand in the shade, and its blood cooled back down.

WHOMP!

HOW UNDIGNIFIED!

The sails were stiff and didn't fold down, so these creatures must have had to be careful not to stand sideways in a strong wind.

Dimetrodon

Ophiacodon

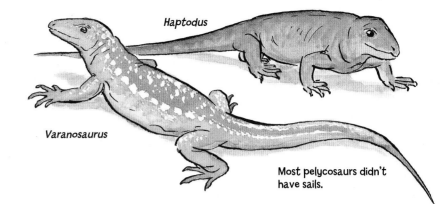

Haptodus

Varanosaurus

Most pelycosaurs didn't have sails.

Pelycosaurs like *Dimetrodon* and *Ophiacodon* were the fiercest carnivores the world had yet seen, preying on other large animals. Others, like *Varanosaurus* and *Haptodus*, probably ate smaller prey, including bugs. There were also large pelycosaur plant-eaters. Remember all those plant-covered uplands (and lowlands)? They provided a nonstop veggie buffet for these vegetarians, and no one was more into it than a group called the caseids. The caseids became big blob-shaped eating machines. To judge by their huge bodies and tiny heads, they must have been both slow and dim-witted, which makes one wonder how they managed not to get eaten. Maybe they were too big to bother with, or maybe they tasted really, really bad—there is much fossil bones will never tell us.

Cotylorhynchus, a large caseid

CASEIDS AT THE DINER

WOULD YOU FOLKS LIKE SEED-FERN OR REGULAR?

DUH? DUH?

ARE THESE GUYS DUMB, OR WHAT?

I'LL JUST BRING REGULAR, HOW ABOUT THAT?

All good things must come to an end, and eventually a new group of carnivorous synapsids emerged called therapsids. Apparently the first thing on their "to do" list was either to out-compete the pelycosaurs or have them for lunch. After eating the last of the synapsid plant-eaters, some of the therapsids themselves became vegetarians, and the first large land animal food chain was born: lots of herbivores turning plants into meat, and a smaller number of carnivores preying on them.

The most common herbivores by far were porky little guys called dicynodonts. They had a horny beak instead of front teeth, and some of them lived in burrows in the ground, woodchuck-style. There were also big, lumbering plant-eaters like *Moschops*. *Moschops* had a thick, rocklike skull. Scientists think it was the world's first head-butter. Since head-butting is usually done by social animals to establish who's boss, it may mean that *Moschops* lived in herds the way modern bison do.

Moschops

Diictodon,
a dicynodont

The carnivorous therapsids in the meantime were becoming more and more mammal-like. Dog-size *Lycaenops* was one example. It stood higher off the ground than earlier synapsids (which helped it run better), and looked like what you would get if you crossed a lizard with a German shepherd.

Lycaenops

Even more mammal-like was *Procynosuchus*. *Procynosuchus* showed signs of a faster, warmer metabolism. For one thing, it could breathe and chew at the same time, thanks to a shelf separating the inside of its nose from its mouth. This was important because as a more active, warm-blooded animal, it needed to chop up its food so it could digest it more quickly. Reptiles, on the other hand, generally swallow their meals down whole, holding their breath as they do so. So it's thanks to these Permian innovators that we can chew gum without turning blue! Another improvement was having different teeth for different jobs: little front ones for snipping, fangs for ripping, and back teeth for slicing and dicing.

Procynosuchus, 2 ft (60 cm) long. We can't know for sure, but it may well have had fur to help keep it warm.

THAT LADY IS YOUR GREAT-GREAT-GRANDMOTHER, AND THIS FELLOW OVER HERE IS YOUR GREAT-GREAT-GREAT-GREAT-GREAT ... WELL, YOU GET THE IDEA!

LATE P.M., LATE PERMIAN

It's a peaceful late afternoon 250 million years ago in what is now South Africa. Two *Arctognathus*, big therapsid meat-eaters, are soaking up the last rays of sun on a ledge overlooking a wide floodplain. Several amphibians called *Rhinesuchus* are basking on the sandbars in the river below. On the far bank a herd of *Dicynodon* is browsing among the horsetails. *Glossopteris* grows on the higher spots that don't get flooded too often, and the hilltops are covered in pines.

Nothing in the scene gives any clue as to what's about to happen next.

BEEP!

BEEP!

BEEP!

LADIES AND GENTLEMEN, AN EMERGENCY BROADCAST— A DEVASTATING EXTINCTION IS UNDER WAY. WE HAVE NO WORD YET AS TO THE CAUSE.

The Mother of All Extinctions

We're in Siberia. Enormous lava flows are creeping over the landscape, scorching everything in their path. Where the lava reaches a lake or a marsh, it boils the water instantly, sending up huge columns of steam. These are the Siberian Traps, where volcanic activity spewed molten rock over an area twice the size of Alaska. Many scientists think the Siberian Traps were one of the main causes of the giant extinction.

With the lava came huge amounts of carbon dioxide (CO_2) and other greenhouse gases. The planet was already hot and dry, and the extra CO_2 turned it into an oven. The oceans became stagnant, with very little oxygen (O_2), which killed most of the sea life. Poisonous gases released from the seafloor by the higher temperatures may have also played a part.

This was the most devastating extinction ever. Only about 10 percent of plant and animal species made it through to the Triassic. Every life-form alive today descends from the handful of tough survivors that went on to repopulate the planet in the next period, the Triassic.

But every end is a new beginning, and in the face of new challenges nature always gets creative. Two groups in particular were in for some big changes. The therapsids, on the one hand, were about to shrink and become true mammals. The archosaurs, on the other hand, were poised to turn into dinosaurs ... so read on! You will find out all about it in *Part III: When Dinos Dawned.*

Part III

WHEN DINOS DAWNED, MAMMALS GOT MUNCHED, & PTEROSAURS TOOK FLIGHT

A Cartoon Prehistory of Life in the Triassic

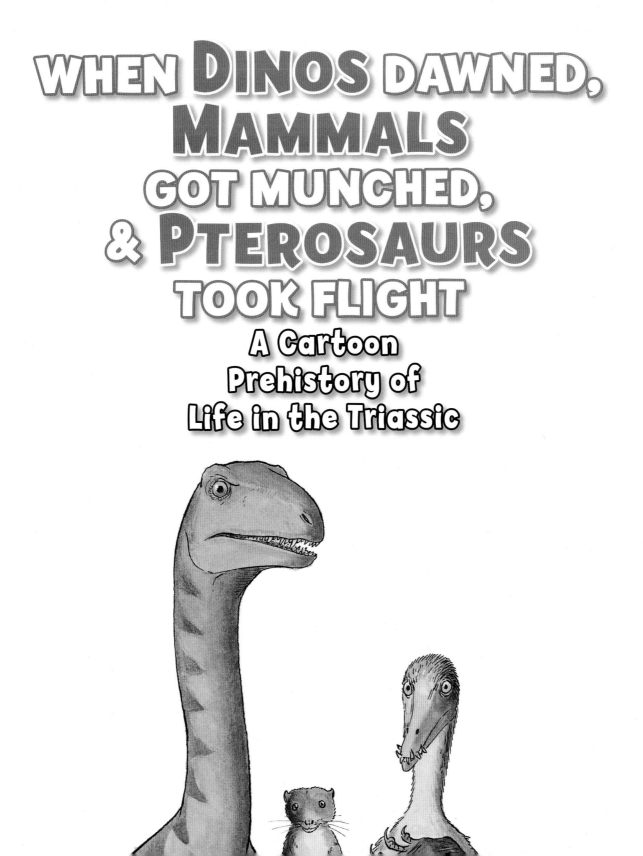

WELCOME TO THE TRIASSIC

It's 7 a.m. in South Africa, at the very beginning of the Triassic period. The day has barely begun, and it's already unbearably hot out. Dozens of *Lystrosaurus*, low-slung animals that look like small pigs, are busy scrunching their way through a stand of corn-size plants called *Pleuromeia*.

MORE SCORCHING WEATHER AHEAD, FOLKS. WE RECOMMEND STAYING IN YOUR BURROWS IN THE MIDDLE OF THE DAY.

Wherever we go in the early days of the Triassic we find the same things: a hot, dry landscape, smallish plants, and lots of *Lystrosaurus* eating them. The planet is struggling to recover from the end-Permian extinction, and while there is a fair amount of life, there is very little variety and a conspicuous absence of anything big. There are no big animals and no big plants; trees and forests are nowhere to be seen.

Lystrosaurus, 3 ft (1 m) long

Thrinaxodon, a cat-size carnivore, 20 in (50 cm) long

The biggest carnivore, *Proterosuchus*, was only about 5 ft (1.5 m) long.

THE RETURN OF THE FORESTS

We're in France, eight million years later. The Siberian Traps have finally stopped belching gases, and life is getting back on its feet. The survivors of the extinction have evolved into many new species. Forests are just beginning to make a comeback. The conifers (the group that includes pines and firs) are doing especially well, and bugs both old and new are crawling among the leaves and buzzing through the warm air.

Mayflies

NEW!

Grauvogelia, the oldest known fly

Triadotypus was a huge dragonfly, with a 1-ft (30-cm) wingspan. The other insects shown were the same size or smaller than their modern relatives.

NEW!

Tiny *Rosamygale* is the earliest known ancestor of tarantulas 1/10 in (2.5 mm) long.

Lots of cockroaches and many kinds of beetles

Assorted leaf-hopper and grasshopper ancestors

Aethophyllum, a small, grassy conifer

The trees are *Voltzia,* a conifer that survived the end-Permian extinction.

Pelourdea, a conifer with long, flat leaves

WORLD'S OLDEST SPECIES!

Eocyclotosaurus, a big amphibian, 6 ft (3 m) long

Three-eyed *Triops cancriformis* is still alive in Europe today.

Dipteronotus, 2 in (5 cm) long

Triops cancriformis, 3 in (8 cm) long

Clytiopsis, a crayfish, 1.5 in (4 cm) long

The Arms Race Is Back

Predators just got bigger, and so did the plant-eaters. In China, for instance, relatives of *Lystrosaurus* such as *Sinokannemeyeria* (an awfully long name—why don't we dub it Potato-face instead?) were the size of a small cow. Stalking two Potato-faces is *Shansisuchus*, a ten-foot (3-m)-long early relative of dinosaurs and crocodiles.

THE TRIASSIC PLANET

The Triassic is the first period of the famous Mesozoic era. Partway through the Triassic, the sea flooded Europe for about ten million years, leaving behind a layer of rock full of fossil seashells sandwiched between two layers of nonmarine rock. A 19th-century German geologist named the Triassic for these three layers. You might have already guessed that the name had something to do with the number three (think of words like *triangle, tricycle,* or *Triops,* the three-eyed crustacean we saw on page 80).

THE CONTINENTS TODAY

NORTH AMERICA
EUROPE
ASIA
AFRICA
SOUTH AMERICA
AUSTRALIA
ANTARCTICA

NORTH POLE

Panthalassa Ocean

SIBERIA

LAURASIA

NORTH AMERICA

EUROPE

NORTH CHINA

SOUTH CHINA

PANGAEA

AFRICA

Near the Equator the climate was very dry, and there were deserts.

EQUATOR

Paleo-Tethys Sea

ARABIA

The continents were all stuck together, forming a giant C-shaped continent called PANGAEA. The northern half is referred to as LAURASIA, and the southern half is called GONDWANA.

SOUTH AMERICA

GONDWANA

INDIA

Farther from the Equator the climate was wetter, and there was more vegetation.

AUSTRALIA

Lystrosaurus fossils have been found at both ends of Pangaea. It was truly a worldwide animal.

ANTARCTICA

It wasn't cold anywhere in the Triassic. Both Poles were ice-free.

SOUTH POLE

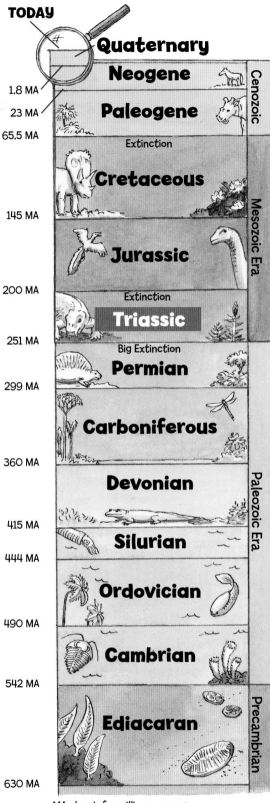

TODAY

Quaternary

Neogene

1.8 MA

Paleogene

23 MA

65.5 MA

Extinction

Cretaceous

145 MA

Jurassic

200 MA

Extinction

Triassic

251 MA

Big Extinction

Permian

299 MA

Carboniferous

360 MA

Devonian

415 MA

Silurian

444 MA

Ordovician

490 MA

Cambrian

542 MA

Ediacaran

630 MA

Cenozoic

Mesozoic Era

Paleozoic Era

Precambrian

MA stands for million years ago.
(In Latin, "million years" is *mega annum*.)

We humans probably wouldn't enjoy a trip to the early Triassic. The air was hot and oxygen levels were lower than what we're used to, so besides sweating like pigs, we might feel a little weak or dizzy. As plants and ocean life recovered, oxygen levels went up, making it a far more appealing destination.

The climate also got wetter over time, with an especially wet period about halfway through the period. Scientists think that for much of the Triassic, intense wet seasons (monsoons) alternated with very dry seasons, and huge storms were common.

Forests grew almost all the way to the Poles, which were too warm to have any year-round ice. Fossil tree trunks from Antarctica have growth rings that show that even though it wasn't cold out, the trees stopped growing in the winter because of the long months of winter darkness.

THE TRIASSIC EXPLOSION

Once ecosystems recovered, life went nuts. So many new plants and animals evolved that some scientists refer to this burst of creativity as the Triassic Explosion. Let's take a look at how the explosion played out among the tetrapods.

Bursting forth from the yellow cloud are the archosaurs and their relatives. From just a few Permian survivors they evolved into a spectacular array of animals including dinosaurs, pterosaurs, and crocodiles. Find out more on pages 90–95, and 105.

Ambling forth from the reddish cloud are our ancestors, the therapsids. They included stocky plant-eaters as well as a line of carnivores that gave rise to the first tiny mammals. More on pages 90–91 and 102–103.

Eudimorphodon

Plateosaurus

Pisanosaurus

Lotosaurus

Coelophysis

Postosuchus

Desmatosuchus

Hyperodapedon

Effigia

Hesperosuchus

Pseudopalatus

Kannemeyeria

Thrinaxodon

Morganucodon, an early mammal

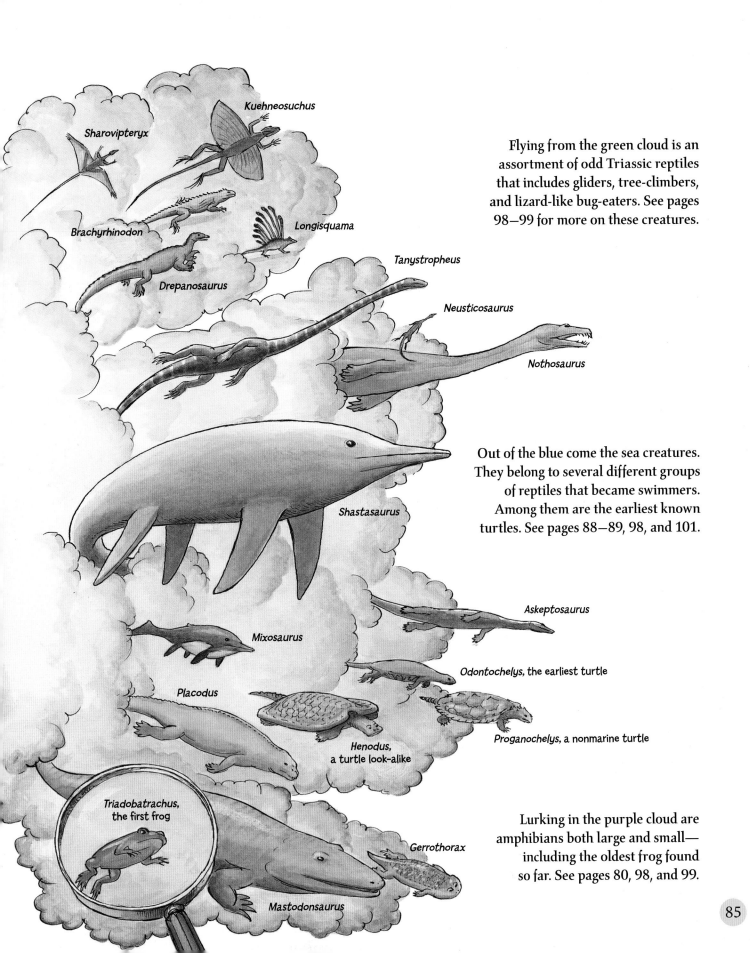

Kuehneosuchus

Sharovipteryx

Brachyrhinodon

Longisquama

Drepanosaurus

Tanystropheus

Neusticosaurus

Nothosaurus

Flying from the green cloud is an assortment of odd Triassic reptiles that includes gliders, tree-climbers, and lizard-like bug-eaters. See pages 98–99 for more on these creatures.

Shastasaurus

Out of the blue come the sea creatures. They belong to several different groups of reptiles that became swimmers. Among them are the earliest known turtles. See pages 88–89, 98, and 101.

Askeptosaurus

Mixosaurus

Odontochelys, the earliest turtle

Placodus

Proganochelys, a nonmarine turtle

Henodus, a turtle look-alike

Triadobatrachus, the first frog

Gerrothorax

Lurking in the purple cloud are amphibians both large and small—including the oldest frog found so far. See pages 80, 98, and 99.

Mastodonsaurus

SUN AND FUN ON THE TETHYS

Of course, the Triassic Explosion didn't happen all at once. It happened gradually, and different plants and animals evolved at different times and in different places.

Let's land on one particular spot on Earth, about a third of the way into the Triassic, and check it out. The Southern Alps, for instance. Uh-oh, where are the mountains? The GPS says they should be right here ... Oh, wait, they haven't been pushed up yet. Instead, we're on the shore of the Tethys Sea, gazing at clear tropical waters dotted with islands and reefs. All the ingredients of a summer paradise are here: lush green vegetation, long sand beaches, seashells ... and a leopard-size reptile called *Ticinosuchus* scavenging the stinky carcass of a marine reptile called *Cymbospondylus.* Hmm, I guess the Tethys Tourism Bureau still has some kinks to iron out!

Bjuvia looks like a banana tree but is really a type of seed plant called a cycad.

Conifers

Ptilozamites belongs to an extinct group of seed plants.

Lepocyclotes, a spore plant, is related to *Pleuromeia.*

Protrachyceras, an ammonite, is a shelled relative of squid, up to 1 ft (30 cm) across.

TETHYS TRAVEL

COME SKI IN THE ALPS!

We have the FASTEST nothosaurs at unbeatable prices!

BEACHCOMBERS' HEAVEN

SNORKEL IN THE REEFS!

After a 12-million-year gap, reefs are back! Come see sponges, shellfish, algae, cement-like minerals, and a few corals (for true coral reefs, please come back later in the Triassic).

STARFISH TOURS

TETHYS TRAVEL

BEACHES ARE BACK!

Now that reefs have returned, we have lovely sand made up of bits and pieces of the reef-builders. Come and enjoy!

Ticinosuchus,
10 ft (3 m) long

Cymbospondylus,
up to 30 ft (10 m) long

87

MARINE MADNESS

Underwater, a revolution was taking place that affected the entire food chain, from plankton all the way to top predators. The oceans offered up a fantastic seafood buffet, and a host of new marine reptiles were ready to eat it.

Placodonts specialized in eating shellfish. *Placodus* had buck teeth in front for grabbing clams and big flat teeth farther back for crushing them.
6.5 ft (2 m) long

Nothosaurus,
10 ft (3 m) long

Related to the placodonts were the nothosaurs. They ranged from large, like *Nothosaurus*, to tiny, like *Neusticosaurus.*
10 in (25 cm) long

Clams and other bivalves became very common. Some avoided getting eaten by burrowing into the mud or sand.

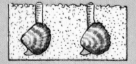

The first oysters

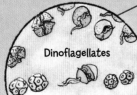

Dinoflagellates

Coccolithophores

Several new kinds of plankton evolved.

SEAWATER DIP

The first lobsters

Cephalopods (squid and ammonites) were very common.

Fish were coming up with many new models, including the earliest flying fish.

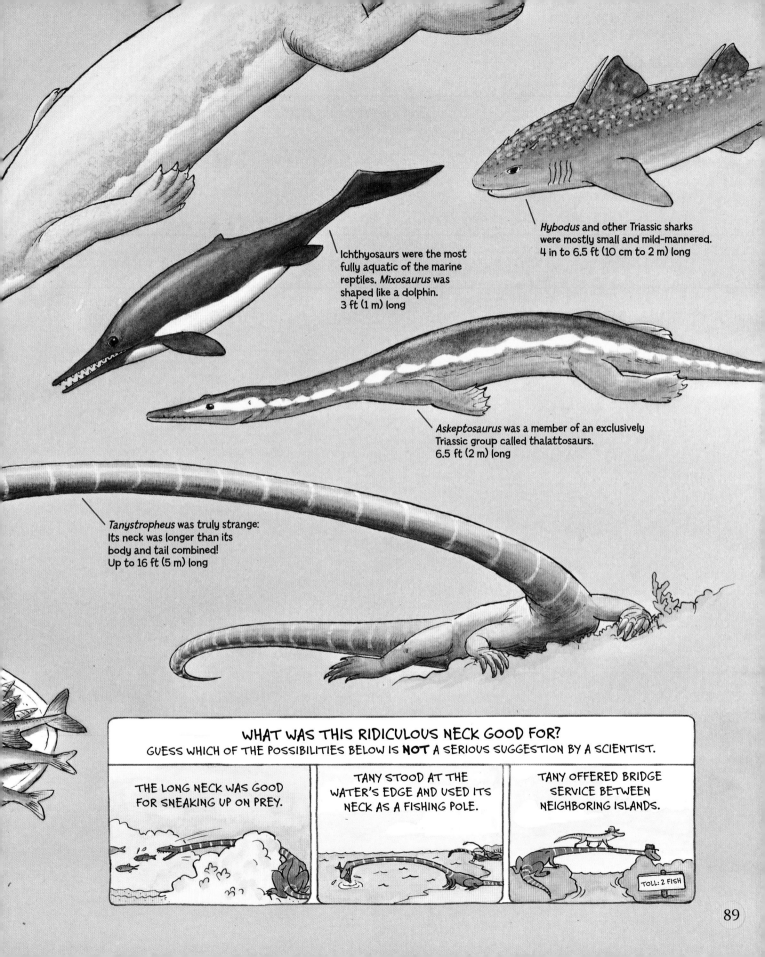

Ichthyosaurs were the most fully aquatic of the marine reptiles. *Mixosaurus* was shaped like a dolphin.
3 ft (1 m) long

Hybodus and other Triassic sharks were mostly small and mild-mannered.
4 in to 6.5 ft (10 cm to 2 m) long

Askeptosaurus was a member of an exclusively Triassic group called thalattosaurs.
6.5 ft (2 m) long

Tanystropheus was truly strange: Its neck was longer than its body and tail combined!
Up to 16 ft (5 m) long

WHAT WAS THIS RIDICULOUS NECK GOOD FOR?
GUESS WHICH OF THE POSSIBILITIES BELOW IS **NOT** A SERIOUS SUGGESTION BY A SCIENTIST.

THE LONG NECK WAS GOOD FOR SNEAKING UP ON PREY.

TANY STOOD AT THE WATER'S EDGE AND USED ITS NECK AS A FISHING POLE.

TANY OFFERED BRIDGE SERVICE BETWEEN NEIGHBORING ISLANDS.

TOLL: 2 FISH

LORDS OF THE LAND

We visited the shore of the Tethys Sea a few pages back. Now let's go farther inland. We're in Argentina, in a broad valley that occasionally gets dusted with ash from nearby volcanoes.

The *Dinodontosaurus* below look familiar, don't they? They are related to *Lystrosaurus* and to our friends the Potato-faces. These creatures are therapsids. So is *Massetognathus,* seen scratching itself on the left (fleas hadn't evolved yet, but biting midges had!). You and I are therapsids as well: If you look at the chart on the right, you will see that this is the branch that led to mammals, including us.

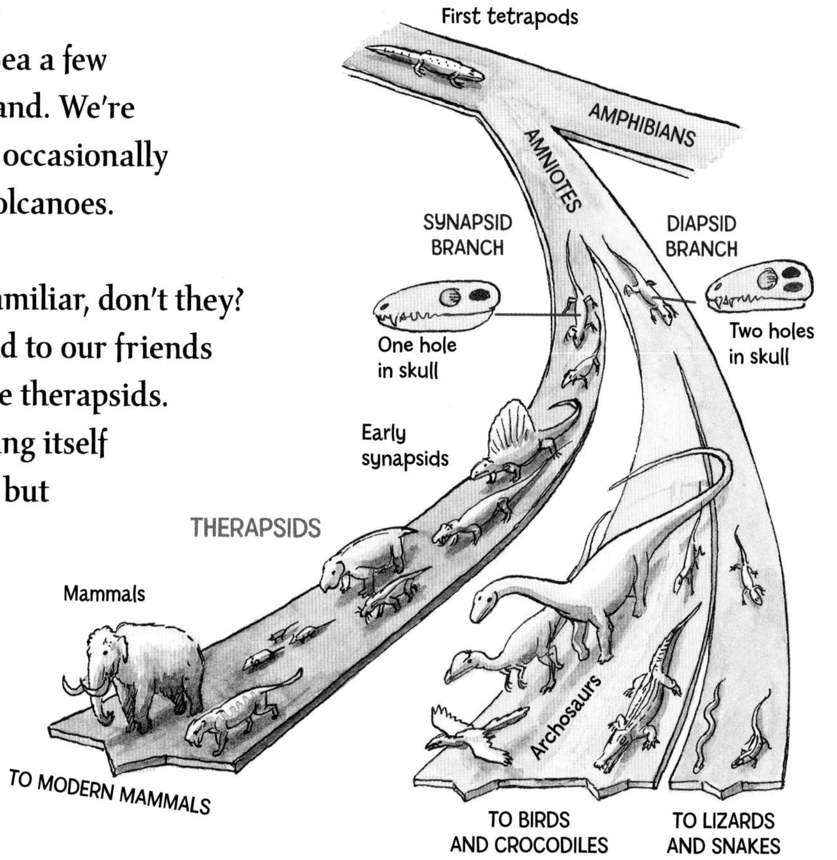

First tetrapods

AMPHIBIANS

AMNIOTES

SYNAPSID BRANCH

DIAPSID BRANCH

One hole in skull

Two holes in skull

Early synapsids

THERAPSIDS

Mammals

Archosaurs

TO MODERN MAMMALS

TO BIRDS AND CROCODILES

TO LIZARDS AND SNAKES

Massetognathus, 3 ft (1 m) long

Marasuchus, 1.7 ft (50 cm) long

The therapsids and their ancestors were the world's most successful land animals in the Permian and in the early Triassic, but now their reign was coming to an end: Archosaurs (the group of reptiles that includes dinosaurs, crocodiles, and birds) were on the rise, poised to steal the crown from the therapsids.

We see two archosaur upstarts in the scene below. One is the tiny *Marasuchus,* an early cousin of dinosaurs (bottom of page 90). The other is *Luperosuchus,* a crocodile relative and top predator that is clearly looking forward to taking over the world one plump therapsid at a time (bottom of this page).

SOME LYCOPOD, YOUR HOMELINESS?

KING THERAPSID'S COURT

LEAVE ME ALONE! IT'S **MY** CROWN!

C'MON! YOU'VE RULED FOR 160 MILLION YEARS—NOW IT'S MY TURN TO RULE FOR 160 MILLION YEARS.*

*Sure enough, 160 million years later the dinosaurs bit the dust, and mammals, the descendants of therapsids, took over the planet once again. Will we be returning the crown to the descendants of birds and crocodiles 95 million years from now? It would only be fair!

Dinodontosaurus, up to 8 ft (2.4 m) long

Luperosuchus, 11 ft (3.5 m) long

THE ARCHOSAURS TAKE OVER

What a difference 20 million years can make! We're now in Arizona, and the place is swarming with archosaurs. The therapsids haven't disappeared entirely, but they're a lot less common than before.

Early in the Triassic, the archosaurs had split into two branches, the dinosaur branch and the crocodile branch. The crocodile branch got off to a quicker start than the dinosaur branch, and for millions of years croc relatives were more common and much more varied than their dino-branch cousins.

DIAPSIDS

NON-ARCHOSAUR DIAPSIDS

ARCHOSAURS

Two holes in skull

The archosaurs added two new holes to their skull for a total of four holes.

DINOSAUR BRANCH

CROCODILE BRANCH

Postosuchus,
13 ft (4 m) long

Hesperosuchus,
4 ft (1.2 m) long

The Ruling Crocs

The crocodile branch produced a crazy number of different creatures, including many dinosaur look-alikes. We saw a few of them, such as *Postosuchus*, *Effigia*, and *Lotosaurus*, back on the Triassic Explosion page. Bet you thought they were dinos, eh?

Postosuchus and other similar meat-eaters were the top predators in their environments. They had tyrannosaur-like heads, but unlike tyrannosaurs they had front legs that could still be used for walking, at least part-time.

Phytosaurs like *Pseudopalatus* were crocodile look-alikes, but were not the direct ancestors of modern crocodiles. Oddly enough, the true ancestors of crocodiles were slender, land-dwelling creatures such as *Hesperosuchus*.

The strangest of the bunch were the aetosaurs: Think reptile with a hint of armadillo and a whiff of pig. Aetosaurs were well armored, and they ate plants and possibly grubs and anything else they could root out with their little shovel-shaped snouts.

THE COURT OF THE CROC KING

Pseudopalatus, a phytosaur, up to 20 ft (6 m) long

Typothorax, an aetosaur, 8 ft (2.4 m) long

DINOSAURS DAWN

Dinosaurs at last! It's about halfway through the Triassic, and we've landed back in Argentina to find that a medium-size dino predator, *Herrerasaurus,* is busy ripping apart an unfortunate little fellow dinosaur called *Panphagia.*

Fossils of early dinosaurs are quite rare. When dinosaurs first appeared, other archosaurs were still a lot more common. So were an odd bunch of archosaur cousins called rhynchosaurs. Here we see one, *Hyperodapedon,* slinking off in the hopes of not being noticed by *Herrerasaurus.*

The dinosaurs quickly split into three groups. *Herrerasaurus* belongs to the theropod line, which went on to produce *T. rex* and other monster meat-eaters. And who do you think the gigantic long-necks such as *Brachiosaurus* descended from? Believe it or not, from puny creatures like the unfortunate *Panphagia.* Small though *Panphagia* was, scientists can tell from its teeth and bones that it was indeed a very early member of the sauropod line.

EARLY ARCHOSAURS

CROCODILE BRANCH

DINOSAUR BRANCH

Original hip shape

Saurischians keep original shape.

New hip shape in Ornithischians

Ornithischians

Saurischians

TO STEGOSAURS, DUCKBILLS

TO THE LONG-NECKS

Sauropods

Theropods

TO TYRANNOSAURS, BIRDS

Pterosaurs

Hyperodapedon, 5 ft (1.5 m) long

Exaeretodon, 6.5 ft (2 m) long

One of the earliest known ornithischian dinosaurs, *Pisanosaurus*, is also from Argentina. It too was small and unassuming compared to later ornithischians such as stegosaurs and duckbills. All ornithischians, including *Pisanosaurus*, were vegetarians.

Pisanosaurus,
3 ft (1 m) long

Another Triassic first were the pterosaurs. The pterosaurs were the first tetrapods to truly fly. These distant relatives of dinosaurs appeared on the shores of the Tethys in the late Triassic, but they didn't become common until later, in the Jurassic.

MAN, THAT CROWN WOULD LOOK **SO** GOOD ON ME!

ZZZ

A DINOSAUR IN THE CROC KING'S COURT

Eudimorphodon,
wingspan,
3.2 ft (1 m)

Herrerasaurus,
14.5 ft (4.5 m) long

Panphagia,
about
5 ft (1.5 m) long

MUNCH, MUNCH, MUNCH, PLANTS FOR LUNCH

What were all these new creatures eating? Let's go back to South Africa about halfway through the Triassic to find out. We're in the same spot where *Lystrosaurus* was munching on *Pleuromeia* on page 78, only now the vegetation is lush and incredibly diverse.

Most of the trees and shrubs you see are gymnosperms, plants that make seeds but not flowers. They include conifers, cycads, ginkgos, and an extinct group called seed ferns (which are not ferns, despite their name). In fact, the only plants in sight that are not gymnosperms are the ferns and horsetails by the river, which are spore plants.

What you won't see are flowers. Flowering plants didn't take off until the Cretaceous period. As a result, on Valentine's Day the poor inhabitants of Pangaea had to give one another bunches of pinecones instead.

Beetles in flight

There was a huge variety of beetles, just like in our modern forests.

NEW!

Early ancestors of moths and butterflies

Dicroidium was a seed fern that grew all over the southern half of Pangaea.

CHIRP CHIRP CHIRP

NEW!

Crickets

Kannaskoppia, a seed fern, had berry-like seeds.

A variety of tiny beetles nibbled on cycad cones and pollen.

The leaf litter was full of cockroaches.

Pseudoctenis, a cycad

A Bug Buffet

Scientists have found oodles of insect fossils among the plants. They have also found the fossilized remains of munched and tunneled leaves, chewed-out logs, nibbled cones, and other evidence that by the middle of the Triassic, insects had perfected every possible plant-eating technique.

WE GOT MORE WAYS TO EAT A FOREST THAN ANY BUG THAT CAME BEFORE US. WE EAT POLLEN, WE DRINK SAP, WE DO THE HUNGRY INSECT RAP.

WE CAN BURROW, WE CAN SWIM, WE EAT LOGS OUT FROM WITHIN. WE EAT LEAVES AND TENDER SHOOTS, WE EAT SEEDS AND MUNCH ON ROOTS.

WE GOT MORE WAYS TO EAT A FOREST THAN ANY BUG THAT CAME BEFORE US. WE EAT POLLEN, WE DRINK SAP, WE DO THE HUNGRY INSECT RAP!

True bugs (insects with special sucking mouthparts) were also common.

Heidiphyllum was a conifer with long, flat leaves instead of needles.

Dicroidium trees

Ferns

Equisetites, a horsetail

97

Drepanosaurus had a prehensile tail and a huge claw on each hand. It may have ripped open bark to get at beetle larvae. Italy. 16 in (40 cm) long

Closely related *Megalancosaurus* was a bit like a modern chameleon. Italy. 10 in (25 cm) long

Tiny *Hypuronector* may have lived in the trees or in the water. U.S.A. 4.7 in (12 cm) long

ANOTHER POSSIBLE USE FOR MEGALANCOSAURUS'S TAIL HOOK ...

... AND HYPURONECTOR'S WIDE TAIL.

A MARVELOUS MENAGERIE

Let's not forget the smaller creatures! Here are some of the strange beings that the Triassic cooked up to take advantage of all those bug-filled treetops above and the equally enticing bug- and fish-filled ponds below.

Some of these creatures were related to the archosaurs, and others to our modern lizards and snakes (except for the little frog next to the pond, which is, of course, an amphibian).

Odontochelys, the oldest known turtle. China. 16 in (40 cm) long

Tanytrachelos was a tiny freshwater relative of super-long-necked *Tanystropheus*. U.S.A. 12 in (30 cm) long

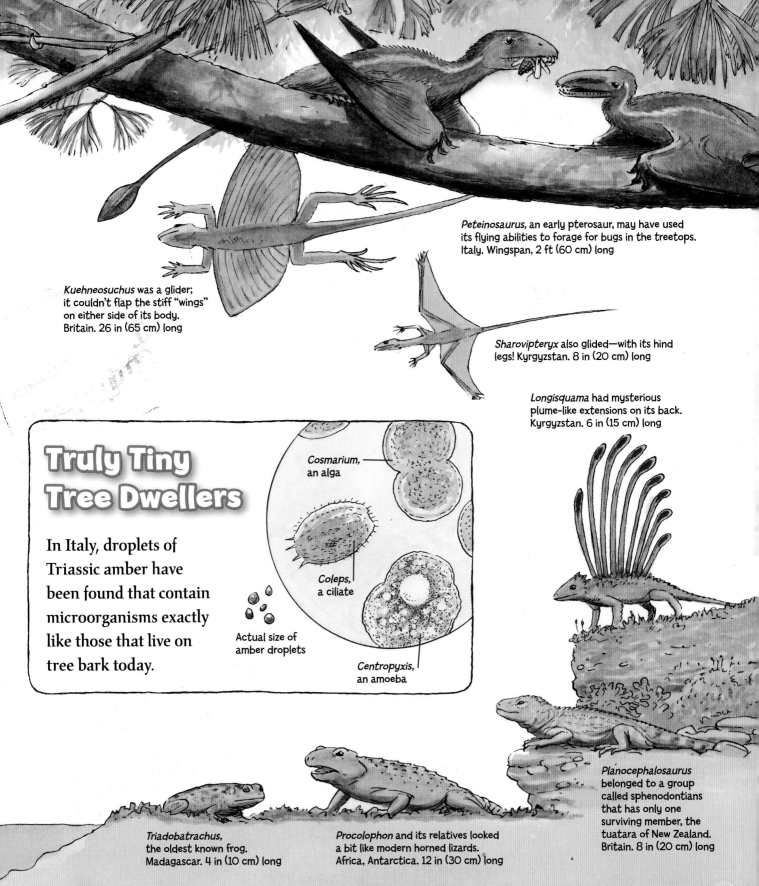

Peteinosaurus, an early pterosaur, may have used its flying abilities to forage for bugs in the treetops. Italy. Wingspan, 2 ft (60 cm) long

Kuehneosuchus was a glider; it couldn't flap the stiff "wings" on either side of its body. Britain. 26 in (65 cm) long

Sharovipteryx also glided—with its hind legs! Kyrgyzstan. 8 in (20 cm) long

Longisquama had mysterious plume-like extensions on its back. Kyrgyzstan. 6 in (15 cm) long

Truly Tiny Tree Dwellers

In Italy, droplets of Triassic amber have been found that contain microorganisms exactly like those that live on tree bark today.

Cosmarium, an alga

Actual size of amber droplets

Coleps, a ciliate

Centropyxis, an amoeba

Planocephalosaurus belonged to a group called sphenodontians that has only one surviving member, the tuatara of New Zealand. Britain. 8 in (20 cm) long

Triadobatrachus, the oldest known frog. Madagascar. 4 in (10 cm) long

Procolophon and its relatives looked a bit like modern horned lizards. Africa, Antarctica. 12 in (30 cm) long

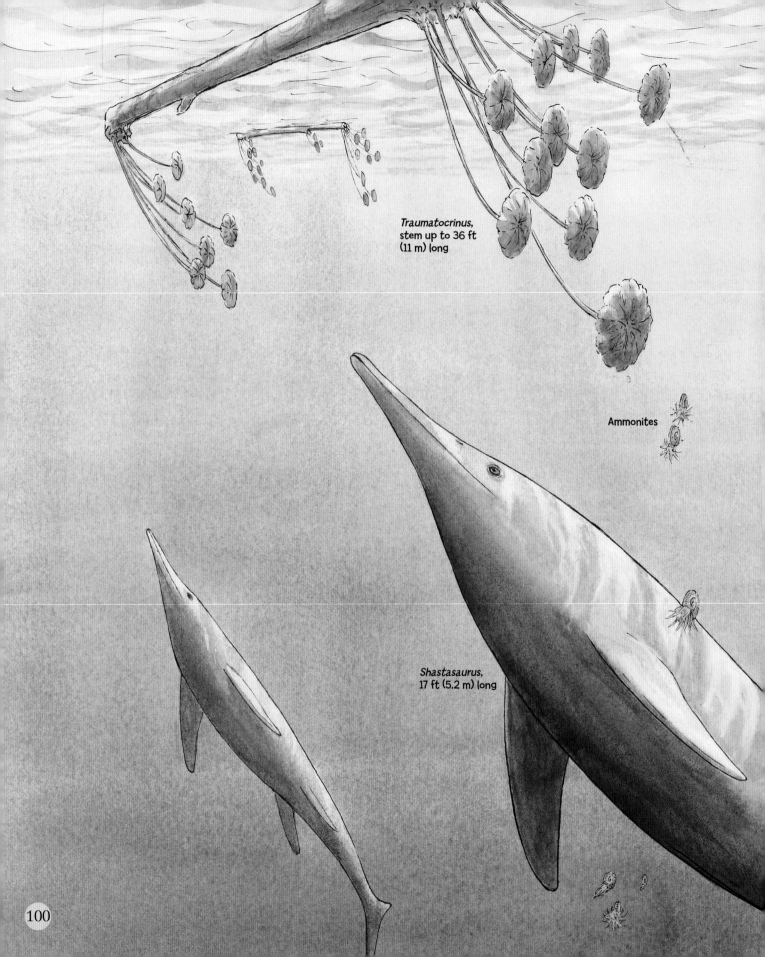

Traumatocrinus,
stem up to 36 ft
(11 m) long

Ammonites

Shastasaurus,
17 ft (5.2 m) long

A Sea Change

What was happening underwater in the meantime? Let's go snorkeling in the seas of southern China in the late Triassic to find out.

Dangling above us are crinoids, flower-shaped relatives of starfish. Normally crinoids live attached to the seafloor, but *Traumatocrinus* grew on bits of driftwood. Their feathery arms acted as nets to trap plankton as the wind pushed their driftwood rafts along.

Gliding along below are two large ichthyosaurs called *Shastasaurus.* Fear not! The *Shastasaurus* will probably ignore you; they normally eat squid and other small prey.

First Coral Reefs

Modern reef-building corals first appeared in the Triassic. They owe their tremendous success to ... sugar farming! Just as humans grow sugar beets or sugarcane, these corals trap and grow countless dinoflagellates (see page 88) under their "skin." The dinoflagellates are photosynthetic, meaning that they use sunlight to turn water and carbon dioxide into sugars. The corals eat these sugars to supplement what they can catch with their tentacles. The corals' waste products in turn fertilize the waters around them, which is why coral reefs are so incredibly full of life.

MORPHING INTO MAMMALS

We're in what is now England, peering into the rocky home of *Morganucodon,* an early mammal. Later British mammals drank tea and ate scones, but these mouse-size animals ate bugs instead, and they did so at night rather than in the afternoon. There were plenty of insects out at night, and more important, there were fewer predators. Many dinosaurs and other meat-eaters hunted by day.

Mammals didn't just appear out of nowhere. Various small therapsids became more and more mammal-like, to the point where the line between "almost-but-not-quite-mammals" and true mammals is often a little blurry. Most scientists agree that "Morgie," as *Morganucodon* is affectionately known, was indeed a true mammal. How about you? Take the test to find out.

ARE YOU A MAMMAL?
Standardized Test – Valid for All Pangaea

INSTRUCTIONS: If alive, complete whole test. If you are extinct, skip Part I since soft-tissue evidence doesn't fossilize well.

PART I

1. Do you stay at a constant temperature on the inside (unless you have a fever)? .... YES ☐ NO ☐

2. Do you have hair and/or peach fuzz anywhere on your body? .... YES ☐ NO ☐

3. Does your skin produce any of the following: sweat, grease, peculiar smells? .... YES ☐ NO ☐

4. Do you have mammary glands (breasts) or at least nipples? .... YES ☐ NO ☐

PART II

5. Is your lower jaw made up of a single bone, the dentary? (Hint: A reptile has several bones in its lower jaw.) .... YES ☐ NO ☐

6. Do you have teeth of different shapes for nipping, slicing, and chewing? .... YES ☐ NO ☐

7. Do you have three middle-ear bones, instead of just one, like reptiles? If you don't know, answer this instead: Can you hear high-pitched, squeaky sounds? .... YES ☐ NO ☐

If you answered "yes" to all questions, you are a certified mammal.

First Dairy Products, First Fur?

Today's mammals have live babies and suckle their young. What about Morgie? We can look for clues in the duck-billed platypus, one of our most primitive living mammals. It lays eggs, and it doesn't exactly suckle its young. Instead, milk oozes onto the fur on its belly, and the babies lap it up. Triassic mammals may have laid eggs and oozed milk as well.

It is very likely that early mammals were at least somewhat warm-blooded, or endothermic, meaning that they generated heat from within. Morgie and its relatives probably had fur to help keep the warmth in, but we don't know what this fur looked like.

"ARTISTIC LICENSE"

WHEN I RECONSTRUCT AN ANIMAL, I LIKE TO CONSULT DIRECTLY WITH MY SUBJECT.

IS THIS WHAT YOUR FUR WAS LIKE, MORGIE?

BRRRR! MORE HAIR!

LIKE SO?

YES, YES, KEEP GOING!

WAAAAIT A MINUTE!

You probably know the rest of the story. Our ancestors stayed small and dino-phobic for the rest of the Mesozoic, and it paid off: They took over the planet when the dinosaurs went extinct 150 million years later.

Lilientsernus,
16 ft (5 m) long

Plateosaurus,
up to 33 ft (10 m) long

A Changing World

It's the rainy season in Germany, 205 million years ago. At the edge of a forest, two fast-moving *Liliensternus* are converging on a small group of *Plateosaurus.* The adult *Plateosaurus* has just heard them and has raised its head, but the theropods are unlikely to attack such a large animal: It's the younger *Plateosaurus* they're after.

Plateosaurus and other early long-neck dinosaurs were the biggest animals on Earth so far, and they could browse higher up in the trees than earlier plant-eaters. The theropods were also getting bigger, and dinosaurs were now the most common big animals on the planet. Even so, in many places massive crocodile-branch meat-eaters continued to be the top predators.

QUEEN DINO'S COURT

The Triassic is almost over. Will it have a happy ending? Grab a sandwich, sit down at your desk, click your mouse (or your tiny early mammal, since rodents haven't evolved yet), and take a look at the online news to find out ...

Proganochelys,
23 in (60 cm) long

| HOME | TODAY'S NEWS | VIDEO | MOST POPULAR | SPORTS |

The Late Triassic Times.com
Wednesday, April 21, 205 MA

HEARTBREAK IN PANGAEA

Rumors have surfaced that North America and Africa are beginning to drift apart. A tearful Africa declared, "We are seriously considering going our separate ways. It's sad, but after 80 million years, we're a little sick of each other."

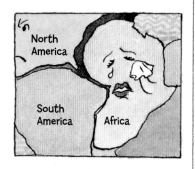

END OF AN IDYLL

In similar news to the south, there are rumors of a possible rift between South America and its neighbors, North America and Africa.

PANGAEA'S BROKEN HEART
A GLOBAL THREAT

Scientists are concerned that where there once was love, there may soon be lava. The rift between the continents is opening cracks in the Earth's crust. Huge amounts of lava could spill out, along with CO_2 and other gases, and endanger life on the planet.

DINOSAURS TAKE OVER,
says Census Bureau

According to 205 MA census figures, dinosaurs are now the planet's most successful land animals, ahead of other archosaurs.

Census figures show very few mammals, but many may have gone uncounted due to their shy nocturnal habits and their fear of the mainly carnivorous census-takers.

Census-taker at work

WEATHER

TODAY	THURSDAY	FRIDAY
99°	102°	103°

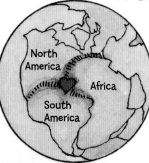
106

EXTINCTION SANDWICH

The Triassic ended with another big extinction. Once again, volcanic activity is one of the main suspects. This time lava flowed from where Pangaea was beginning to break up into separate continents. The result was a less deadly version of the end-Permian extinction.

Many marine creatures died. On land, the plants didn't do too badly. Mammals survived (obviously, or you wouldn't be reading this), and so did the dinosaurs and pterosaurs. The crocodile relatives weren't so lucky: Only the crocodiles themselves survived. The moment the curtain lifted on the next period, the Jurassic, the dinosaurs looked around, saw they had the place to themselves, and immediately grew bigger and meaner, becoming the true rulers of Pangaea. But that's a whole other story!

THE END

A Time Line of Life on Earth

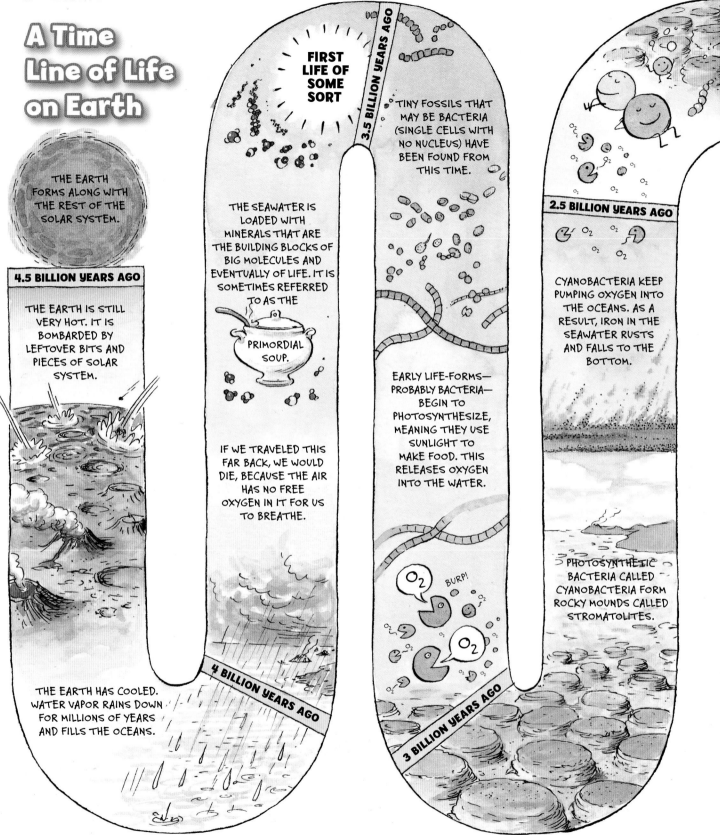

THE EARTH FORMS ALONG WITH THE REST OF THE SOLAR SYSTEM.

4.5 BILLION YEARS AGO

THE EARTH IS STILL VERY HOT. IT IS BOMBARDED BY LEFTOVER BITS AND PIECES OF SOLAR SYSTEM.

THE EARTH HAS COOLED. WATER VAPOR RAINS DOWN FOR MILLIONS OF YEARS AND FILLS THE OCEANS.

4 BILLION YEARS AGO

THE SEAWATER IS LOADED WITH MINERALS THAT ARE THE BUILDING BLOCKS OF BIG MOLECULES AND EVENTUALLY OF LIFE. IT IS SOMETIMES REFERRED TO AS THE PRIMORDIAL SOUP.

IF WE TRAVELED THIS FAR BACK, WE WOULD DIE, BECAUSE THE AIR HAS NO FREE OXYGEN IN IT FOR US TO BREATHE.

FIRST LIFE OF SOME SORT

3.5 BILLION YEARS AGO

TINY FOSSILS THAT MAY BE BACTERIA (SINGLE CELLS WITH NO NUCLEUS) HAVE BEEN FOUND FROM THIS TIME.

EARLY LIFE-FORMS— PROBABLY BACTERIA— BEGIN TO PHOTOSYNTHESIZE, MEANING THEY USE SUNLIGHT TO MAKE FOOD. THIS RELEASES OXYGEN INTO THE WATER.

O_2 BURP!

O_2

3 BILLION YEARS AGO

2.5 BILLION YEARS AGO

CYANOBACTERIA KEEP PUMPING OXYGEN INTO THE OCEANS. AS A RESULT, IRON IN THE SEAWATER RUSTS AND FALLS TO THE BOTTOM.

PHOTOSYNTHETIC BACTERIA CALLED CYANOBACTERIA FORM ROCKY MOUNDS CALLED STROMATOLITES.

BACTERIA ARE STILL THE ONLY LIFE-FORMS.

WHEN THERE IS NO MORE IRON LEFT FOR THE OXYGEN TO ATTACH TO, OXYGEN STARTS TO ESCAPE INTO THE ATMOSPHERE.

O_2 O_2 O_2 O_2 O_2 O_2 O_2 O_2 O_2 O_2 O_2 O_2 O_2 O_2 O_2

2 BILLION YEARS AGO

THE OZONE LAYER FORMS AND PROTECTS LIFE FROM TOO MUCH HARMFUL ULTRAVIOLET RADIATION.

BACTERIA STILL RULE.

FIRST SEXUAL REPRODUCTION: SOME CELLS COMBINE THEIR CHROMOSOMES WITH THOSE OF ANOTHER CELL INSTEAD OF JUST SPLITTING IN TWO. THIS SPEEDS UP EVOLUTION.

CERTAIN BACTERIA BECOME SPECIALIZED PARTS INSIDE THESE LARGER CELLS.

FIRST NONBACTERIAL CELLS APPEAR. THEY ARE BIGGER AND MORE COMPLEX, AND THE CHROMOSOMES ARE PACKAGED IN A NUCLEUS.

1.5 BILLION YEARS AGO

HMPH!

1 BILLION YEARS AGO

THE FIRST MULTICELLULAR ANCESTORS OF PLANTS AND ANIMALS APPEAR.

EARLY VERSIONS OF OUR MODERN CONTINENTS START TO FORM.

DRY LAND IS ALMOST TOTALLY LIFELESS.

PRECAMBRIAN

630 MA

TODAY!

QUATERNARY
MODERN HUMANS

1.8 MA

NEOGENE

PALEOGENE
MAMMALS TAKE OVER.

CENOZOIC

65 MA

Extinction

CRETACEOUS
FLOWERING PLANTS

JURASSIC
FIRST BIRDS, LOTS OF DINOSAURS

MESOZOIC

Extinction

SEE PART III
Pg. 79

TRIASSIC
FIRST DINOSAURS, FIRST MAMMALS

251 MA

Big Extinction

PERMIAN

SEE PART II
Pg. 45

CARBONIFEROUS

PALEOZOIC

DEVONIAN

SEE PART I
Pg. 11

SILURIAN

ORDOVICIAN
EARLY PLANTS. LOTS OF SEA LIFE, EARLY FISH

CAMBRIAN
SEAS FILL WITH NEW ANIMAL FORMS.

EDIACARAN
STRANGE, SOFT-BODIED SEA ANIMALS

542 MA

MA = MILLION YEARS AGO

109

Our Vertebrate Family Tree

TREES WITHIN TREES

Here are the main branches of our vertebrate family tree. In reality, every bit of the tree contains other smaller trees. For instance, if you were to research the bird branch, you would see different bird groups splitting off over time, with some going extinct, like the giant Moa, and others surviving to our day. If I wanted to show all the branches, I would need to draw a chart the size of a king-size bed sheet!

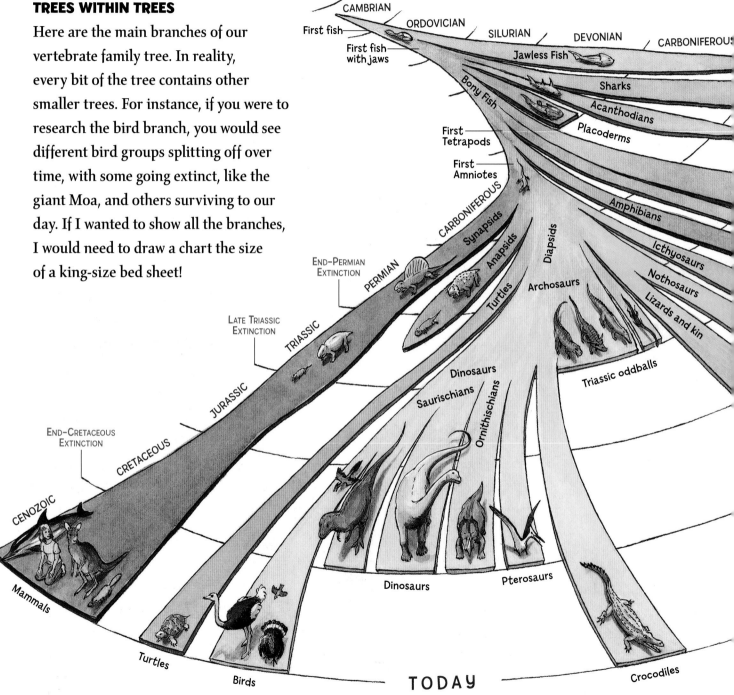

CAMBRIAN
ORDOVICIAN
SILURIAN
DEVONIAN
CARBONIFEROUS

First fish
First fish with jaws
Jawless Fish
Bony Fish
Sharks
Acanthodians
Placoderms
First Tetrapods
First Amniotes
Amphibians
Icthyosaurs
Nothosaurs
Lizards and kin
CARBONIFEROUS
Synapsids
Anapsids
Diapsids
END-PERMIAN EXTINCTION
PERMIAN
Turtles
Archosaurs
Dinosaurs
Triassic oddballs
LATE TRIASSIC EXTINCTION
TRIASSIC
Saurischians
Ornithischians
JURASSIC
END-CRETACEOUS EXTINCTION
CRETACEOUS
CENOZOIC
Mammals
Turtles
Birds
Dinosaurs
Pterosaurs
Crocodiles
TODAY

110

Lampreys and Hagfish

Sharks

Jawless fish

Sharks and rays

Ray-fins

Lobe-fins

Coelacanths and Lungfish

Ray-fin fish

Lobe-fin fish

Icthyosaurs and kin

Amphibians

Nothosaurs and kin

Frogs and salamanders

Lizards and snakes

TROUBLE WITH TURTLES

Scientists agree on the main branches of the tree, but some of the details may change over time as they discover new fossils and use new techniques for comparing genes to figure out who's related to whom. As I write this, paleontologists are busy trying to decide where turtles belong. Do they descend from the anapsid branch? It would make sense, since like ancient anapsids, turtles have no holes in their skulls (see page 66). But scientists who have compared the genomes of turtles and of other living reptiles claim that turtles belong to the diapsid ("two-hole") branch. According to this theory, turtles originally had two holes in their skull but lost them over time. For now I've put them with the diapsids on the family tree, but who knows whether they'll stay there!

Activities: Our Vertebrate Family Tree

How can it be that animals as incredibly different as sharks, frogs, and kangaroos all evolved from the same fishy early vertebrates way back in the Cambrian? You can explore this and more with the following activities based on the family tree we just saw on the previous page. The activities are independent; you can do several of them or just focus on one.

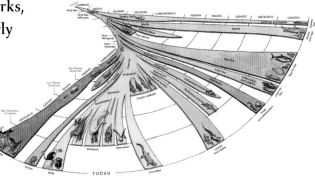

Activity 1

BE AN ANIMAL

Choose to be a member of one of the living groups of vertebrates. You could be anything: a goldfish, a newt, an eagle, an alligator, a bear ... any animal you wish. Then describe when your group first appeared, who your ancestors are, and who you are most closely related to. If you're doing this at school, you can then talk to a classmate and find out how you're related. If, for example, you are a coyote and your pal is an iguana, who is your common ancestor? A common ances- tor is the kind of animal that existed just before your respective branches of the family tree split apart.

THAT LADY IS YOUR GREAT-GREAT-GRANDMOTHER AND THIS FELLOW OVER HERE IS YOUR GREAT-GREAT-GREAT-GREAT-GREAT ... WELL, YOU GET THE IDEA!

Activity 2

FROM SCALES TO FUR: THE SYNAPSIDS

Look at our mammalian heritage. It's worth writing, telling, or singing (why not?) the epic tale of our glorious, if not always beautiful, ancestors, the synapsids. Your readers/audience will be surprised to hear that our synapsid ancestors were the dominant land animals for many millions of years until the dinosaurs took over. Describe the origins of synapsids and how and when they eventually became mammals. You'll find lots of information about them in parts II and III of this book. And if you think I'm being unfair regarding their looks, please consider species such as *Moschops* and *Lycaenops* (pages 70–71) or *Sinokannemeyeria* (left and page 81).

Activity 3
ARE YOU A MAMMAL?

Take the test on page 102. Once you've determined whether you're a mammal, make up a new test for one of the other groups. The test can have many questions or very few. Suggestions: "Are you an amphibian?" "Are you a shark?" "Are you an ichthyosaur?" You can use any of the other groups on the family tree. If you want a challenging one, write up "Are you a dinosaur?" and then see if a bird would pass the test, since birds are the descendants of dinosaurs. Good luck—this is a tricky one! Birds may or may not pass the test because they've specialized for eons for a very different lifestyle.

Activity 4
A GHOST COMES TO LIFE: YOU DISCOVER A LIVING FOSSIL

Imagine that you and your colleagues are digging for fossils in a hidden valley in China, in the foothills of the Himalaya. To your amazement, near your campsite you discover a living reptile that looks like nothing you have ever seen before. Back in the lab, your colleagues agree that this is a surviving aetosaur (see page 93). Everyone thought they'd gone extinct at the end of the Triassic! Since it has continued to evolve and to adapt to its small mountain valley habitat, this living fossil no longer looks much like its Triassic ancestors. Have fun imagining this fictional new discovery. Draw a picture and write a short description of it. Include its length, type of teeth, likely diet, and other details. Give the animal a Latin name, since the discoverer of a new species gets to name it. Remember: Capitalize the first (genus) name, but not the second (species) name. If there's a bunch of you, you can each choose a different kind of extinct animal from the family tree. It might be fun to invent a living pterosaur, for instance, or a dinosaur, or a small nothosaur that has survived in a lake in the valley (or a large one that has survived in a deep lake in Scotland ... Sound familiar?).

Activity 5
SWIMMERS AND FLIERS

1 You can see from the family tree that birds and crocodiles are more closely related to one another than they are to the rest of the living groups: They have a common archosaur ancestor in the late Permian. Can you think of some reasons why they are so very different looking?

2 Ichthyosaurs and dolphins, on the other hand, look very similar. How can you tell them apart? How closely related are they? Why is their overall shape so similar?

Activity 6
THERE'S SOMETHING FISHY IN OUR FAMILY'S DISTANT PAST

This is a more open-ended thinking activity of the sort that leads scientists to come up with new ideas. Looking at the family tree, write down everything that comes to mind, whether it's things that seem obvious, things you had no idea about, relationships that seem surprising, groups that went extinct ... anything. You might come up with questions that the family tree doesn't answer. You will most likely be able to sleuth out the answers somewhere in the book, unless they have to do with animal groups that split ways later than the end of the Triassic. If you can't find the answers anywhere, you may need to become a paleontologist and do research in order to answer them.

Activity 7
HOW FISH GOT FEET

Describe the transition from fish to four-legged animals. You will find the information in part I of this book, and also by going online to an excellent University of Chicago website about *Tiktaalik*, the amazing "fishapod" from Ellesmere Island, at tiktaalik.uchicago.edu. The site includes lots of clearly explained information about the fossil itself and about how it was discovered, as well as a Q&A (question and answer) section and a list of good resources for further research. Please always check in with a teacher, librarian, or parent before going onto the Web.

Activities: Geological History Time Line

The first activity is short and sweet. The second activity is a major group endeavor, but one that, besides being fun and resulting in an exhibit that others can enjoy, will give you an idea of the jobs and the teamwork involved in putting together real-life science exhibits. And bringing the time line to life on a big scale is a good way to (sort of, kind of, maybe) grasp the enormous spans of geological time.

Activity 1
EVOLVE OR PERISH

Play the board game Evolve or Perish, available in color or in black and white at mnh.si.edu/ete/ETE_Education&Outreach_Game.html. Print it out, find some dice, and you're all set to move through the last 635 million years Chutes and Ladders—style. I created this game with scientists at the Smithsonian. Note: It's cheaper to print black and white, and you or your siblings may enjoy coloring it in.

created by Hannah Bonner, Cindy Looy, Ivo Duijnstee and other members of the ETE program of the National Museum of Natural History, Smithsonian Institution

Activity 2 THE WALL OF TIME

Using a roll of craft paper, put up an illustrated time line on a long wall. Use as reference one of the time lines in the book (see page 83). The Evolve or Perish game (see left) can also help. If there is a very long wall to fill and sufficient interest, the time line can be like the one on pages 108–109, and include the full history of life.

First, get together and decide who does what, and plan the sequence of tasks. I suggest the following teams and jobs:

EXHIBIT DESIGNERS AND COORDINATORS

You will be the overall designers of the exhibit, put up the paper, draw the long line of the time line itself, make aesthetic decisions, and be in charge of materials throughout the whole process. Discuss the total length of the time line with the geologist team below. Leave space at the end for "creative add-ons." I suggest using craft paper on a long wall (gym, hallway, outdoor school wall), but if no wall is available, you can do a simpler version in chalk on the ground outdoors.

GEOLOGISTS: CALCULATE THE TIME LINE

Use math to figure out where to place the MA (millions of years) markers bracketing the periods. If the available wall is x feet long, and the time line is 635 million years, figure out the scale. Once the time line is

up, your team helps make sure images and text are placed in the right time frame.

PALEONTOLOGISTS: PLACE FOSSIL ANIMALS AND PLANTS

Add points showing the appearance of the first marine invertebrates, the first land animals (arthropods), and the first insects. Show when fish first appeared, and when each major group of vertebrates branched off. Also place the first land plants, the first trees, and the first seed plants. Place the first flowering plants in the Cretaceous and the spread of grasslands in the Neogene. These last two events are not covered in the main text of this book but are shown on the time line on pages 108-109.

GEOLOGISTS/PALEONTOLOGISTS: PLOT PLANETARY EVENTS

Locate and show when the principal extinctions took place (three in the book, plus the end-Cretaceous one, which finished off the dinosaurs). Point out on the time line when there was ice at the Poles and when the planet was warm all over. Check with an adult, then print out paleomaps from the Paleomap Project at scotese.com (click on Earth History). Put these up in the corresponding spots on the time line.

SCIENTIFIC ILLUSTRATORS: ILLUSTRATE THE TIME LINE

Draw some animals and plants that lived in each period. You can also print out images

from the Web, but you'll learn a whole lot more if you draw them yourself. You can draw or paint directly onto the time line, or on separate pieces of paper that you then stick onto the time line. The last periods, from the Jurassic to today, are not covered in this book, but you shouldn't have any trouble finding images of these periods in other books.

CREATIVE ADD-ON

Leave room to add the Anthropocene at the end. The Anthropocene is the current era, in which humans are having a huge effect on the planet. You could even include a Post-Anthropocene (or any name you care to make up—I just made this one up) with its corresponding paleomap. The Scotese website includes maps many millions of years into the future. It's very interesting to see what scientists predict continental drift will do. The illustrators among you can have fun drawing imaginary future plants and animals that the rest of you envision. You even get to decide how long our species will survive, or what it might morph into. Other creative add-ons could be acting out events from the time line, or composing raps or poems or songs about various events (see the rap on page 97—bet you can do better!).

WHEN YOU'RE DONE Invite the rest of your school to admire your work and be there to answer questions other kids may have.

Activities: Climate Change and Extinctions

These three activities involve some research and some creative thinking.

Activity 1
EXTINCTIONS: WHOSE FAULT WERE THEY?

Put on your paleodetective hat and figure out who was to blame for the following extinctions:

1 The late Devonian extinction in part I
2 The devastating end-Permian extinction at the end of part II
3 The end-Triassic extinction at the end of part III

Were the culprits the same in all three? Were they all climate related? You will find most of your answers in the pages of this book. "Extra Info: Paleoclimates" on page 117 can give you some additional insights into what drives climate change. And now for an optional bonus question:

4 What about the most famous extinction of all, the one that killed off the dinosaurs at the end of the Cretaceous? It's not part of this book, but you can find information on it in many books about prehistoric life.

Activity 2
SURVIVORS

How come some species of plants and animals survive an extinction, and others don't? Answering the following questions will give you some clues.

● Are life-forms that are highly specialized for a particular lifestyle more or less likely to survive than adaptable, I'm-happy-anywhere species?

● The characters below are pleased to have survived the end-Permian extinction. In this case, do you see any species that had adaptations that happened to come in handy when conditions suddenly changed?

● To judge by the plants and animals living just after the extinction (see page 79), would you say that body size played a part in their survival? Did any very large animals or plants survive?

Now you're ready to tackle Activity 3.

Activity 3
THE DEMISE OF THE DINOSAURS

Can you think of some reasons why the dinosaurs went extinct at the end of the Cretaceous, but crocodiles, birds, and mammals survived? Warning: Scientists are still scratching their heads over this one, so if you have any brilliant ideas, let your science teacher know.

I WAS ALREADY USED TO HOT WEATHER AND EATING TOUGH PLANTS BEFORE THE EXTINCTION.

Lystrosaurus

WE FUNGI LOVE EATING DEAD STUFF, SO WE DID JUST FINE.

Fungi

ROT ROCKS! WE'RE BACTERIA, AND WE WERE HAPPY AS CLAMS!

Bacteria

I LIVE IN UNDERGROUND BURROWS, AND THAT HELPED ME STAY COOL.

Thrinaxodon

WELL, I'M A CLAM AND I WAS NOT HAPPY! THE OCEANS WERE SO ACIDIC I HAD A REALLY HARD TIME MAKING MY SHELL!

Clam

I WAS JUST PLAIN LUCKY: THE HIGH MOUNTAIN VALLEY I LIVED IN STAYED COOL AND DAMP.

Procolophon

ME? I'M JUST PLAIN TALENTED! I CAN GROW IN FULL SUN OR IN POOR LIGHT, IN WET OR DRY SOIL. AND SEE THESE CHUBBY FEET? THEY'RE FULL OF FOOD IN CASE I NEED IT.

OH, AND I CAN ALSO JUGGLE AND PLAY THE CONCERTINA!

Pleuromeia

SURVIVORS OF THE END-PERMIAN EXTINCTION

You'd be surprised how much paleontologists and geologists know about ancient climates. There's even a specialized field of study called paleoclimatology. We now know that many forces drive our Goldilocks planet toward hot, cold, or just-right conditions. There are three major kinds of climate drivers: geological forces, life forces, and astronomical forces.

GEOLOGICAL FORCES

WANDERING CONTINENTS

Are the continents separate, or are they stuck together in larger units? This affects many things, including ocean circulation, which controls how water distributes heat around the planet.

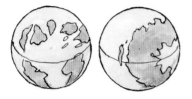

Are colliding continents shoving up mountain ranges? When rain falls over newly exposed rock, it takes CO_2 from the air and binds it to minerals in the rocks. This lowers CO_2 in the atmosphere and cools the planet.

Where are the continents in relation to the Equator and the Poles? This also affects climate. For example, if new mountains are forming in a hot, rainy place near the Equator, they will weather much faster (and cool the planet more) than they would in a cold, dry place near the Poles.

VOLCANOES

Volcanoes can both cool and warm the planet. They spew out particles that block sunlight and cool the planet for a short time, but they also release CO_2, which stays in the atmosphere for a long time, warming the planet for hundreds of years.

LIFE FORCES

COOL VEGETATION

When there's lots of vegetation photosynthesizing and creating thick soils, the CO_2 that plants take from the air ends up as carbon in the soil. As a result, CO_2 goes down in the atmosphere, cooling the planet. Photosynthesis in the oceans can also lower CO_2 and cool things down.

GREENHOUSE GASES

But life can also do the opposite: When cattle burp, ponds bubble with marsh gas, or we burn fossil fuels or forests, two greenhouse gases, CO_2 and methane, return to the atmosphere and the planet warms up.

ASTRONOMICAL FORCES

SUNSPOTS AND AXIS TILTS

There are many astronomical forces, and they can be quite complex. A few examples are sunspots, which affect how much solar radiation reaches the Earth, and slight variations in the tilt of the Earth's axis and in the shape of its orbit around the sun.

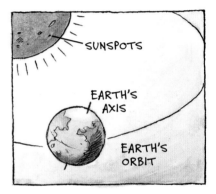

We also have asteroids colliding with the planet from time to time. Most asteroids are small and fairly harmless, but the occasional big ones can have dramatic effects. Just ask the dinosaurs!

FEEDBACK LOOPS

There are also all kinds of feedback loops affecting climate. One example is something called the albedo effect: When there is a lot of ice at the Poles, the frozen white surface bounces sunlight back out of the atmosphere, and the planet cools even more. As the ice melts, the opposite happens: The darker ocean water absorbs more sunlight and the planet warms up even more.

Activities: Paleo Reconstruction

RECONSTRUCTING ANIMALS

Here's how to do a simple two-dimensional reconstruction of an animal from a drawing of the skeleton. In this example, I'm using the skeleton of *Herrerasaurus*, the early dinosaur on page 95.

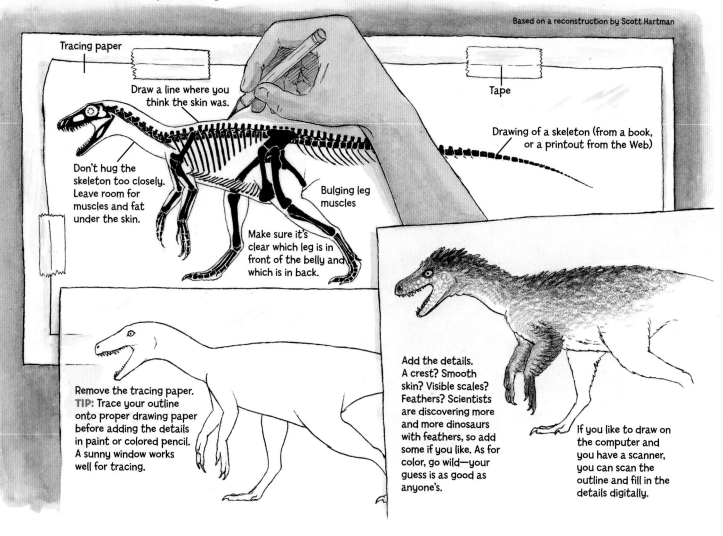

Based on a reconstruction by Scott Hartman

Tracing paper

Draw a line where you think the skin was.

Don't hug the skeleton too closely. Leave room for muscles and fat under the skin.

Bulging leg muscles

Make sure it's clear which leg is in front of the belly and which is in back.

Tape

Drawing of a skeleton (from a book, or a printout from the Web)

Remove the tracing paper.
TIP: Trace your outline onto proper drawing paper before adding the details in paint or colored pencil. A sunny window works well for tracing.

Add the details. A crest? Smooth skin? Visible scales? Feathers? Scientists are discovering more and more dinosaurs with feathers, so add some if you like. As for color, go wild—your guess is as good as anyone's.

If you like to draw on the computer and you have a scanner, you can scan the outline and fill in the details digitally.

RECONSTRUCTING PLANTS AND LANDSCAPES

If you want to put your animals in a scene, you'll need to draw plants. You'll find plenty of examples throughout the book. Photos of modern plants can serve as inspiration, especially photos of forests in the Pacific Northwest of the United States, where ferns grow beneath huge conifers, a combination that was common in the Mesozoic. Remember that flowering plants did not become common until the mid-Cretaceous.

TIP: Just because there wasn't any grass doesn't mean the ground was bare! Other low-growing plants covered the ground: ferns, small extinct seed ferns, grassy conifers (like *Aethophyllum* on page 80), mosses, lichens, and more created carpets of greenery.

Exercise 1: TRY IT OUT!

Once you've reconstructed this creature below, try to find it in the book.
(If you give up, the answer is at the bottom of the page.)

TIP: Remains of bony scales tell us it was scaly, not feathery.

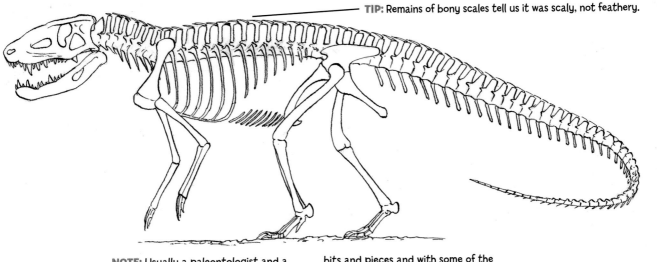

NOTE: Usually a paleontologist and a scientific illustrator work together to reconstruct a skeleton. It's not easy, since fossil skeletons are often found in bits and pieces and with some of the bones missing. It's thanks to their work that we can come up with lifelike reconstructions of prehistoric beasts.

Exercise 2: PRACTICE MAKES PERFECT

Now do the same thing with this skeleton of a living animal. **HINT:** It's a mammal that is common in North America and has black markings around its eyes. You're going to have to draw lots of fur!

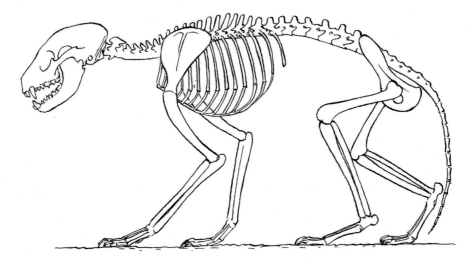

From the Author: Brain Popcorn

Sometimes when I'm researching stuff for a book I'll come across a new concept, and when I grasp it fully for the first time, there's this nice sensation in my brain, a sort of expanding "poof!" as if a kernel of brain had just popped. I thought I'd share a few of my favorite bits of brain popcorn with you.

THE CELLULOSE CHALLENGE: WILL THE TRUE HERBIVORES PLEASE STAND UP?

I used to think I understood the basic food chain on land: herbivores (whether bugs or four-legged animals) eat plants, and carnivores eat the herbivores. Then as I was researching part I, I learned that when land plants first evolved, no one was in a hurry to eat them. Bugs ate only rotten leaf litter, and turned up their noses, or rather their antennae, at anything green and salad-like. First tetrapods? Same thing. They ate bugs and fish, but not greenery. First reptiles? Same story: They ate bugs. The earliest mammals? You guessed it: insectivores. Each group had to evolve for a while before it added some vegetarians to its ranks. This really had me scratching my head. Plants are plentiful and extremely easy to catch: Why not eat them?

It turns out that the only way herbivores can make use of cellulose, which is the main ingredient in plant stems and leaves, is if microbes do the digesting for them. This is why the earliest bugs ate rotten plants (see page 25) that had been "predigested" by bacteria and fungi. Every time a new animal group decided to start eating plants, they had to set up a composting bin in their gut and invite a whole bunch of microbes to come live there, ferment the cellulose, and turn it into food for them. This is what cows, horses, gorillas, iguanas, and all other modern herbivores continue to do today, and what the great long-neck dinosaurs did on a truly grand scale in the Mesozoic.

So if the true herbivores were to stand up, we wouldn't be able to see them: They're microscopic!

NOTE: When humans eat vegetables, we digest sugars and other nutrients, but we don't digest the cellulose: It's what we call "dietary fiber," and it passes right through us. We have gut bacteria that help us digest other things, though.

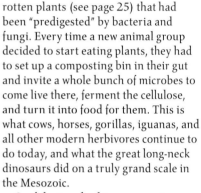

GYMNOWORLD

When I was researching the plants that grew in South Africa in the Triassic for the landscape on pages 96–97, I was blown away by the fact that diversity was really high, in spite of the fact that there was not a single flowering plant. The nonflowering seed plants, known scientifically as gymnosperms, were in high gear until flowering plants began to take over in the Cretaceous. Today the conifers, some cycads, a few other plants, and a single species of ginkgo are all that is left of this once huge group.

We humans are true flower children, because our primate ancestors evolved after the rise of flowering plants. All the plants we eat—fruits, nuts, vegetables, beans, grains, sweeteners—come from flowering plants. Warning: If you are a vegetarian, avoid time-traveling to any time earlier than the Cretaceous. You would most likely die of hunger!

A MINI-ACTIVITY:

Try to think of at least two foods we can eat that come from gymnosperms, or nonflowering plants. If you're not sure which plants are gymnosperms, check page 96.

(In case you come up empty-handed, answers are at the bottom of the page.)

1) pine nuts, 2) fiddleheads (the tender shoots of certain ferns), 3) melinjo (Indonesian chips made from a plant called *Gnetum*), and 4) ginkgo tree nuts

COUSIN GOLDFISH

A goldfish is more closely related to you than it is to a shark! Goldfish and humans both evolved from early bony fish, whereas sharks are cartilaginous fish.

ANIMALS ARE OLDER THAN PLANTS

I always thought that plants came first, but actually animals appeared in the oceans long before some intrepid algae turned into the first plants and colonized the land.

SCIENCE CHANGES

1 In this case I didn't exactly learn something new, but I did become much more aware of something I already knew: that science changes as new discoveries or insights get published. In general this is great—it's what makes science exciting and constantly self-improving—but in this case I was a teensy bit annoyed. Soon after *When Bugs Were Big* first appeared, the same scientists who had published a paper describing the giant spider *Megarachne* (page 55) published a new paper basically saying "Oops! We blew it! It's really a eurypterid." Here is the before and after of this creature.

The new *Megarachne*

The old *Megarachne*

2 Another science update has to do with *Tiktaalik* (pages 37–39). *Tiktaalik* was a recent discovery when I wrote *When Fish Got Feet*, and the paleontologists still hadn't found the hind portion of the animal. They've since extracted *Tiktaalik*'s hindquarters from the rocks they'd collected. The pelvis turns out to be surprisingly sturdy, indicating that *Tiktaalik* could propel itself along the bottom using all four fins.

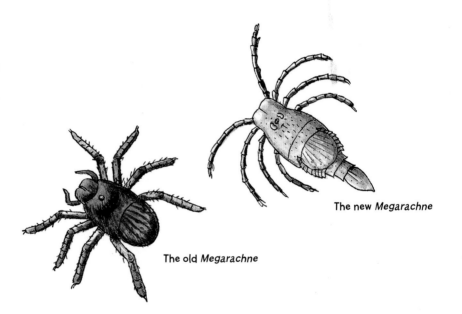

Tiktaalik as I drew it before its pelvis was discovered

Tiktaalik with its newly discovered pelvis in place

Where to Learn More

BOOKS

National Geographic Kids Ultimate Dinopedia by Don Lessem, with illustrations by Franco Tempesta. National Geographic, 2010. Chock full of information. Also available as an iPad app.

The Concise Dinosaur Encyclopedia by David Burney, with illustrations by John Sibbick. Kingfisher, 2004. It starts with the Cambrian and has a brief but very good chapter on each of the periods leading up to the Mesozoic.

History of Life by Richard Cowen. Wiley-Blackwell, 2013. A college-level textbook that's easy to follow and fun to read thanks to the author's easygoing and often humorous style.

Prehistoric Life: The Definitive Visual History of Life on Earth edited by DK Publishing, 2009. A mega-encyclopedic look at all aspects of the history of life with tons of images and scientifically sound text.

Dawn of the Dinosaurs: Life in the Triassic by Nicholas Fraser. Indiana University Press, 2006. A science book for grown-ups with amazing artwork by Douglas Henderson.

Cruisin' the Fossil Freeway by Kirk Johnson and Ray Troll. Fulcrum Publishing, 2007. A funny, articulate paleontologist and a zany artist embark on a road trip to visit fossils of the American West and tell the story in this wonderful all-ages book.

Ancient Denvers: Scenes From the Past 300 Million Years of the Colorado Front Range by Kirk Johnson and friends. This little booklet can be ordered from the Denver Museum of Nature and Science. It has the absolute best paintings of scenes from Denver's deep past, based on the plants and climate of each period. The first three scenes are from the time frame of this book; the rest are Jurassic to present.

Prehistoric Journey by Kirk Johnson and Richard Stuckey. Denver Museum of Natural History/Roberts Rinehart Publishers, 1995. A very readable and profusely illustrated overview of ancient life.

How Dinosaurs Came to Be by Patricia Lauber, with illustrations by Doug Henderson. Simon and Schuster Books for Young Readers, 1996. A very nice book about Permian and Triassic fauna.

Synapsida: A New Look at the Origin of Mammals by John C. McLoughlin. Viking Press, 1980. A great book and fun to read, with simple black-and-white illustrations that work very well.

WEBSITES

Remember to get adult approval before venturing forth onto the Web.

Palaeos, palaeos.com. Often the best site for an overview of a period, or a particular group of extinct animals, because it is amazingly complete.

The UC Berkeley Museum of Paleontology site, ucmp.berkeley.edu. Has online exhibits and links to other interesting sites.

For maps of the prehistoric world, go to scotese.com, click on "Earth History," and then choose a time period. Ron Blakey's site at cpgeosystems.com is another terrific source for paleomaps.

The absolute best site for learning about life on land and in freshwater in the Devonian is called Devonian Times, devoniantimes.org. It has all sorts of in-depth information that you won't easily find anywhere else, and good links to related sites.

The go-to site for all things *Tiktaalik* is tiktaalik.uchicago.edu.

Roy Beckemeyer's site windsofkansas .com/fossil_insects.html has a link to wonderful reconstructions of dragonflies and other invertebrates by the German Werner Kraus.

The Tree of Life Web Project, tolweb .org, covers both living and extinct life-forms.

palaeo.gly.bris.ac.uk/research.html. This site from the University of Bristol, in England, has good overall information as well as glimpses of the research being done there.

The Paleontology Portal, paleoportal .org, is a great fossil-hunting resource. Click on "Exploring Time and Space" for a map of the U.S. with information on the geology and fossil sites of every state.

Check out artist Ray Troll's funny, wacky site, trollart.com. He creates great surrealistic paleo art, and also music, including such songs as "I Am a Paleobotanist" and "Devonian Blues."

The National Geographic site, nationalgeographic.com, has lots of great information and resources.

OTHER

● **Natural history museums,** of course! Visit one if you can, but if you aren't lucky enough to live near one, you can consult their websites to find out what's in them.

● **Reconstruction resources:** There's a quick dinosaur anatomy primer at skeletaldrawing.com/ anatomy.

Another useful page about reconstruction is australianmuseum.net .au/Preparing-fossils-reconstructing -the-past.

Good resources for landscape inspiration are *Ancient Denvers* (see Books, left) and any book illustrated by Douglas Henderson. Henderson creates scenes that are entirely believable, with great lighting and fallen logs, scraggly plants, leaf litter and other realistic details. Nature is messy!

Glossary

Ammonite: An extinct relative of squid and octopus that had a characteristic coiled shell.

Amniote: A four-legged animal whose babies are protected in a bag of liquid called an amnion until they hatch or are born. This allows amniotes to develop on dry land, unlike amphibians, which have to lay their eggs in water.

Amphibian: A four-legged animal that spends at least part of its life in water, where it lays its eggs.

Arachnids: A group of eight-legged invertebrates that includes spiders, scorpions, ticks, and mites.

Bacteria: Microscopic single-cell life-forms with a distinctive kind of cell wall and no nucleus.

Bug: In this book, "bug" is used in the popular sense to mean insects as well as other terrestrial invertebrates such as spiders, centipedes, worms, and the like.

Cephalopods: A group of marine animals like squid and octopus that have tentacles sprouting from their head region ("cephalopod" means "head-foot").

Chromosomes: Tiny strands inside a cell that contain information for making a new cell.

CO_2: Carbon dioxide, a gas that is present in small amounts in the air. Plants need it in order to breathe. It is one of the greenhouse gases, so called because they trap heat from the sun and make the planet warmer.

Cycad: A kind of gymnosperm, or nonflowering seed plant, that looks like a small palm tree. Cycads still exist in warm climates today.

Delta: A broad marshy area created by a river as it flows out to the sea.

Embryo: An animal in the early stage of development, before being born or hatched. Plants that are still inside the seed are also called embryos.

Fossil: Remains or traces of a living being that over millions of years have turned into stone.

Fungi (singular, fungus): The group that includes mushrooms, yeasts, and molds. Fungi do not photosynthesize and cannot make their own food from scratch as plants can. Instead, they recycle nutrients created by plants and other life-forms.

Ginkgo: A common Mesozoic tree with a characteristic fan-shaped leaf. Only one species, *Ginkgo biloba*, has survived to this day.

Invertebrate: An animal without a backbone.

Larva: The first stage in the life of certain animals. Larvae look very different than the adult animals they'll grow into. Mosquitoes and frogs start out as larvae.

Niche: A particular set of environmental conditions that a species makes use of. For instance, even if two bird species both eat insects, they occupy different niches if one hunts insects by day and the other hunts at night.

Nucleus: A little rounded "bag" inside nonbacterial cells that contains the chromosomes.

Nutrients: Substances such as sugars, proteins, minerals, and vitamins that living beings use to stay alive and grow.

Nymph: Similar to a larva, but looks more like the adult animal. Dragonflies and cockroaches start out as nymphs.

Ozone layer: A layer of ozone (O^3, a form of oxygen with a strong odor) that surrounds the Earth about 10–20 miles (16–32 km) above the surface.

Plankton: Tiny animals and other life-forms that drift in the water and are a source of food for many larger animals.

Scavenger: An animal that eats the remains of dead animals that it finds.

Temperate: A climate that is neither very hot nor very cold.

Ultraviolet radiation: Also known as UV light, it is a form of light that we can't see, but that causes sunburn.

Vertebrate: An animal with a backbone.

How to Pronounce the Scientific Terms in This Book

acanthodian (AH-kan-THOE-dee-an)

Aethophyllum (ee-tho-FILL-um)

Akmonistion (ak-mon-ISS-tee-on)

amblypigid (AM-blee-PIH-jid)

Amphicyrtoceras (AM-fee-SIR-to-ser-us)

Archaeopteris (AR-kee-OP-te-ris)

Archaeopteryx (AR-kee-OP-te-ricks)

Archosaurus (AR-ko-SORE-us)

Arctognathus (ark-tug-NATH-us)

Arthropleura (AR-thro-PLUR-uh)

arthropod (AR-thro-pod)

Ateleaspis (uh-TEE-lee-ASS-pis)

Athenaegis (ath-en-EE-jis)

Autunia (aw-TOO-nee-uh)

Bjuvia (BYOO-vee-ah)

blastoid (BLAS-toid)

Bothriolepis (BAH-three-oh-LEE-pis)

brachiopod (BRAK-ee-oh-pod)

bryozoan (BRY-uh-ZO-an)

Cacops (KAY-kops)

Cambrian (KAM-bree-an)

Canis (KAY-nus)

Carboniferous (KAR-bo-NI-fur-us)

Carcinosoma (KAR-sin-oh-SOH-ma)

caseid (KAY-see-id)

Cenozoic (sen-oh-ZO-ik)

Cheirolepis (ky-roe-LEE-pis)

Cladoselache (klay-doe-SEL-uh-kee)

Climatius (kly-MAT-ee-us)

coccolithophore (coc-co-LITH-o-fore)

Coelophysis (see-luh-FY-sis)

Coelurosauravus (see-lur-oh-sawr-AV-us)

Cordaites (cord-EYE-tees)

Cotylorhynchus (ko-TILE-oh-RINK-us)

Crassigyrinus (crass-ih-jur-EYE-nus)

Cretaceous (kre-TAY-shus)

crinoid (KRY-noid)

cuticle (CUE-tik-ul)

Cymbospondylus (sim-bus-PON-di-lus)

cystoid (SISS-toid)

Dawsonoceras (DAW-sun-oh-SER-us)

Desmatosuchus (des-ma-to-SOO-kus)

Devonian (de-VONE-ee-an)

Diaphorodendron
  (die-AF-or-oh-DEN-dron)

diapsid (die-AP-sid)

Dicroidium (dy-cro-ID-ee-um)

dicynodont (die-SY-no-dahnt)

Diictodon (die-IK-toe-DON)

Dimetrodon (die-MEE-tro-don)

dinoflagellate (DY-no-FLAJ-el-ate)

Diplocaulus (dip-low-CAW-luss)

Discosauriscus (dis-co-sawr-ISS-cus)

Doryaspis (dor-ee-ASS-pis)

Drepanaspis (drep-uh-NASS-pis)

Drepanosaurus (dreh-PAN-o-SAWR-us)

Dunkleosteus (dun-klee-AW-stee-us)

Edaphosaurus (eh-DAFF-oh-SAWR-us)

Ediacaran (EE-dee-AK-ar-un)

Effigia (eh-fih-JEE-uh)

Elkinsia (el-KIN-see-uh)

Elpistostege (el-pis-toe-STEE-ghee)

Eocaptorhinus (ee-oh-cap-ter-HI-nus)

Eocyclotosaurus
  (EE-oh-cy-CLO-tuh-SAWR-us)

Eophalangium (ee-oh-fa-LAN-gee-um)

Errivaspis (air-ih-VASS-pis)

Eryops (AIR-ee-ops)

Eudimorphodon
  (yoo-dy-MOR-foh-don)

eurypterid (yer-IP-ter-id)

Eusthenopteron (yoos-then-OP-ter-on)

Exaeretodon (ex-a-REHT-uh-don

fungi (FUN-guy *or* FUNJ-eye)

fusulinid (FEW-su-LINE-id)

Glossopteris (gloss-OP-ter-iss)

Gondwana (gon-DWON-ah)

graptolite (GRAP-toe-lite)

Greererpeton (greer-AIR-pet-on)

Haptodus (hap-TOE-dus)

Herrerasaurus (He-REH-ruh-SAWR-us)

Hesperosuchus (HES-pe-roh-SOO-kus)

Hibbertopterus (hib-er-TOP-ter-us)

Hovasaurus (hov-a-SAWR-us)

Howittacanthus (how-it-uh-KAN-thus)

Hylonomus (hi-lo-NO-mus)

Hyperodapedon (HY-per-o-DAP-eh-don)

Ichthyostega (ik-thee-oh-STEE-guh)

Janassa (ja-NASS-ah)

Jurassic (jur-ASS-ik)

Kuehneosuchus (KOO-nee-o-SOO-kus)

Lanarkia (la-NAR-kee-ah)

Leclercqia (le-KLER-kee-ah)

Lepidodendron (lep-id-oh-DEN-drun)

Lepidosigillaria
  (lep-id-oh-si-jill-AHR-ee-ah)

Lepocyclotes (lep-o-seye-CLO-tees)

lichen (LY-kun)

Liliensternus (LIH-lee-en-STER-nus)

Limnoscelis (lim-NOSS-e-liss)

liverwort (LI-ver-wert)

Longisquama (lon-jih-SKWAM-uh)

Lotosaurus (LOH-toh-SAWR-us)

Lycaenops (lie-SEEN-ops)

lycopod (LIE-co-pod)

Lystrosaurus (lis-tru-SAWR-us)

Machairaspis (mac-eye-RASS-pis)

Massetognathus
  (MASS-eh-tog-NAYTH-us)

Meganeuropsis permiana
  (MEG-ah-ner-OP-sis per-mee-AN-uh)

Megarachne (meg-uh-RAK-nee)

Mesozoic (meh-zuh-ZO-ik)

Miguashaia (mig-wa-SHY-ah)

Mimia (MIM-ee-ah)

monuran (mo-NUR-an)

Morganucodon (MOR-gu-NOO-kuh-don)

Moschops (MOSS-kops)

nautiloid (NAWT-uh-loid)

Neusticosaurus (noos-tik-o-SAWR-us)

Nothosaurus (noth-uh-SAWR-us)

Odontochelys (o-don-tuh-KEE-leez)

Ophiacodon (oh-fee-AH-ko-don)

Ordovician (or-do-VISH-ee-an)

Orthacanthus (or-tha-KAN-thus)

palaeodictyopteran
  (pay-lee-oh-dick-tee-OP-ter-an)

Palaeotarbus (pay-lee-oh-TAR-bus)

Paleogene (PAY-lee-oh-jeen)

Paleozoic (pay-lee-oh-ZO-ik)

Paliguana (pa-lig-WAN-uh)

Pangaea (pan-JEE-uh)

Panphagia (pan-FAY-jee-uh)

Panthalassa (pan-thal-AH-suh)

Pantylus (pan-TIE-lus)

Paralycopodites
  (pa-ra-lie-koh-po-DIE-tees)

Parameteoraspis
  (pair-uh-MEE-tee-oh-RASS-pis)

pareiasaur (per-EYE-ah-sawr)

Parexus (pa-REX-us)

Pelourdea (pel-OOR-dee-ah)

pelycosaur (PEL-ih-koh-sawr)

Pennsylvanian (pen-sil-VAY-nee-an)

Permian (PURR-mee-an)

Pertica (PURR-tik-uh)

Petrolacosaurus
  (pet-roh-lack-oh-SAWR-us)

Phlebolepis (fleb-oh-LEE-pis)

Phlegethontia
  (FLEG-eh-THON-tee-ah)

phytosaur (FYE-tuh-sawr)

Pisanosaurus
  (pih-ZAN-uh-SAWR-us)

placoderm (PLAK-oh-derm)

Plateosaurus (plat-ee-o-SAWR-us)

Pneumodesmus (new-mo-DES-mus)

Postosuchus (po-sto-SOO-kus)

Procolophon (pro-KAH-luh-fon)

Procynosuchus
  (pro-sy-no-SOOK-us)

Proganochelys (pro-gan-o-KEE-leez)

Protorosaurus (pro-to-ro-SAWR-us)

Prototaxites (PRO-toe-tax-EYE-tees)

Protrachyceras (pro-trak-ih-SER-us)

Pseudopalatus
  (SOO-doe-puh-LAY-tus)

pseudoscorpion
  (sue-doe-SKOR-pee-un)

Psilophyton (si-lo-FIE-tun)

Pterygotus (TER-ih-GO-tus)

Ptilozamites (til-o-zum-EYE-tees)

Pulmonoscorpius
  (pul-moh-no-SCOR-pee-us)

Quaternary (KWA-ter-nair-ee
  or kwa-TER-ner-ee)

Rhacophyton (rak-o-FIE-ton)

Rhinesuchus (rie-ne-SOOK-us)

Rhyniella (rye-nee-EL-uh)

Rhyniognatha
  (rye-nee-ohg-NATH-uh)

Sawdonia (saw-DOE-nee-uh)

Scaumenacia (skow-men-AY-see-uh)

Scutosaurus (skoo-ta-SAWR-us)

Sharovipteryx (shar-o-VIP-ter-ix)

Sigillaria (si-jill-AHR-ee-ah)

Silurian (si-LURE-ee-an)

Sinokannemeyeria
  (SY-no-KAN-uh-my-EH-ree-a)

stomata (stoe-MAH-tuh)

stromatoporoid
  (stroe-muh-TOP-uh-roid)

synapsid (sin-AP-sid)

Tanystropheus (tan-iss-TRO-fee-us)

Tethys (TETH-iss)

Tetraxylopteris (teh-truh-zie-LOP-ter-is)

thalattosaur (ta-LAT-uh-sawr)

therapsid (theh-RAP-sid)

Thrinaxodon (thrin-AX-uh-don)

Ticinosuchus (ti-SEEN-o-SOOK-us)

Tiktaalik (tick-TA-lik)

tracheae (TRAY-kee-uh)

Traumatocrinus (traw-mat-o-CRY-nus)

Tremataspis (trem-ah-TASS-pis)

Triadobatrachus
  (try-AD-o-ba-TRAY-kus)

Triassic (try-ASS-ik)

trigonotarbid (trig-oh-no-TAR-bid)

trilobite (TRY-lo-bite)

Triops cancriformis
  (TRY-ops can-kri-FOR-mis)

Tuditanus (too-di-TAN-us)

Varanosaurus (va-ran-oh-SAWR-us)

Voltzia (VOL-tsee-uh)

Wattieza (wha-TEE-za)

Xenacanthus (zee-na-KAN-thus)

Index

Acknowledgments

A number of scientists generously contributed their time and knowledge to the three books that make up this volume. My wonderful plants advisors were the paleobotanists Bill de Michele and Carol Hotton at the Smithsonian Institution, Evelyn Kustatscher of the Museum of Nature South Tyrol in Italy, and UC Berkeley paleoecologists Cindy Looy and Ivo Duijnstee. I also had help from Heidi Holmes and John Anderson, specialists in the flora of the South African Molteno formation. Geologists David Kidder and John Beck helped with continents, climate, and extinctions. Piero Gianolla, of the University of Ferrara in Italy, gave me a hand with the Triassic. Cary Easterday advised me on terrestrial invertebrates. Joanne Kluessendorf and Don Mikulic guided me through the reconstruction of a Silurian reef in *When Fish Got Feet*. Corwin Sullivan at the Institute of Vertebrate Paleontology in Beijing, China, has been at my virtual side throughout the entire trilogy, contributing to everything from the big picture of how vertebrates evolved to every last detail of what each creature looked like. If Corwin had had his way, every tiniest detail of every vertebrate illustrated would be perfect. It has never been truer that where this is not the case, the mistakes are mine alone.

Many thanks as well to all the scientists and colleagues who provided me with help, including papers, contacts, and answers to my many questions: Josep Antoni Alcover, Kenneth Angielczyk, Bruce Archibald, Analía Artabe, John Bonner, Kay Behrensmeier, Simon Braddy, Robert Carroll, Marcia Ciro, Matt Celeskey, Karen Chin, Amy Davidson, Marlene Hill Donnelly, Jason Dunlop, Flavia Gargiulo, Patricia G. Gensel, Hans Hagdorn, Philippe Janvier, Kirk Johnson, Tyler Keillor, Jozef Klembara, Andrew Knoll, Conrad Labandeira, John Maisey, Carl Mehling, Nik Mills, Kalliopi Monoyios, Dennis Murphy, Mary Parrish, Luis Pomar, Stephen Priestley, Eben Rose, Iván Rojas, and Rich Slaughter. If I have forgotten to list someone, please know that I am very grateful for your help.

Of course, none of this would ever have coalesced into a book without the terrific team at National Geographic Children's Books: editors Jennifer Emmett and Marfé Ferguson Delano, designers David M. Seager and Ruthie Thompson, and the rest of the team have been just fabulous. A special thanks goes to the godmother of the "When" trilogy, Nancy Laties Feresten, whose idea it was to do books about life before the dinosaurs in the first place.

And last but not least, a big thanks from the bottom of my heart to my family and friends for their love, support, and excellent feedback at various stages of the three books that make up this volume.

Selected Author's Sources for Text and Images

BOOKS

Behrensmeyer, Anna K., et al., eds. *Terrestrial Ecosystems Through Time.* Chicago: University of Chicago Press, 1992.

Carroll, Robert. *The Rise of Amphibians: 365 Million Years of Evolution.* Baltimore: The Johns Hopkins University Press, 2009.

Clack, Jennifer A. *Gaining Ground.* Bloomington, IN: Indiana University Press, 2002.

Clarkson, E. N. K. *Invertebrate Palaeontology and Evolution.* Oxford: Blackwell Science, 1998.

Grimaldi, David and Michael S. Engel. *Evolution of the Insects.* New York: Cambridge University Press, 2005.

Janvier, Philippe. *Early Vertebrates.* New York: Oxford University Press, 2003.

Long, John A. *The Rise of Fishes.* Baltimore: The Johns Hopkins University Press, 1995.

Maisey, John G. *Discovering Fossil Fishes.* Boulder, CO: Westview Press, 2000.

Steyer, Sébastien and Alain Bénéteau. *La Terre Avant les Dinosaures.* Paris: Belin, 2009.

Sues, Hans-Dieter and Nicholas C. Fraser. *Triassic Life on Land: The Great Transition.* New York, NY: Columbia University Press, 2010.

Taylor, Thomas N., Edith L. Taylor, and Michael Krings. *Paleobotany: The Biology and Evolution of Fossil Plants, Second Edition.* Burlington, MA: Academic Press, 2009.

Wood, Rachel. *Reef Evolution.* New York: Oxford University Press, 1999.

ARTICLES

Anderson, John M., Heidi M. Anderson, and Arthur R. I. Cruickshank. 1998. "Late Triassic Ecosystems of the Molteno/Lower Elliot Biome of Southern Africa" *Palaeontology,* Vol. 41, Part 3, 387–421.

Cecil, C. Blaine, et al. 2014. "Middle and Late Pennsylvanian Cyclothems, American Midcontinent: Ice-Age Environmental Changes and Terrestrial Biotic Dynamics." *Comptes Rendus Geoscience,* Vol. 346, 159–168.

Daeschler, Edward B., Neil H. Shubin, and Farish A. Jenkins, Jr. 2006. "A Devonian Tetrapod-like Fish and the Evolution of the Tetrapod Body Plan." *Nature,* Vol. 440 (6), 757–763.

DiMichele, William A. and Nelson, W. John 1989. "Small-Scale Spatial Heterogeneity in Pennsylvanian-Age Vegetation From the Roof Shale of the Springfield Coal (Illinois Basin)." *Palaios,* Vol. 4, 276–280.

Dunlop, Jason A., et. al. 2004. "A Harvestman (Arachnida: Opiliones) From the Early Devonian Rhynie Cherts, Aberdeenshire, Scotland." *Transactions of the Royal Society of Edinburgh: Earth Sciences,* Vol. 94, 341–354.

Dunlop, Jason A. 1995. "Gigantism in Arthropods." *Forum of the American Tarantula Society,* Vol. 4 (5), 145–147.

Falkowski, Paul G., et al. 2004 "The Evolution of Modern Eukaryotic Phytoplankton." *Science,* Vol. 305, 354–360.

Grauvogel-Stamm, Léa and Sidney R. Ash. 2005. "Recovery of the Triassic Land Flora From the End-Permian Life Crisis." *Comptes Rendus Palevol,* Vol. 4, 525–540.

Hünicken, Mario A. 1980. "A Giant Fossil Spider (*Megarachne servinei*) From Bajo de Véliz, Upper Carboniferous, Argentina." *Boletín de la Academia Nacional de Ciencias* (Argentina), Vol. 53, 3/4, 317–325.

Kerp, Hans, Michael Krings, and Christian Pott. 2008. "The Carnian (Late Triassic) Flora From Lunz in Lower Austria: Paleoecological Considerations." *Palaeoworld,* Vol. 17, 172–182.

Kidder, David L. and Thomas R. Worsley. 2010. "Phanerozoic Large Igneous Provinces (LIPs), HEATT (Haline Euxinic Acidic Thermal Transgression) Episodes, and Mass Extinctions." *Palaeogeography, Palaeoclimatology, Palaeoecology,* Vol. 295, 162–191.

Kustatscher, Evelyn and van Konijnenburg-van Cittert, Johanna H. A. (2005): "The Ladinian Flora (Middle Triassic) of the Dolomites: Palaeoenvironmental Reconstructions and Palaeoclimatic Considerations." *Geo.Alp,* Vol. 2, 31–51.

Labandeira, Conrad C. 2005. "Invasion of the Continents: Cyanobacterial Crusts to Tree-Inhabiting Arthropods." *Trends in Ecology and Evolution,* Vol. 20 (5), 253–262.

Preto, Nereo, Evelyn Kustatscher, and Paul B. Wignall. 2010. "Triassic Climates—State of the Art and Perspectives." *Palaeogeography, Palaeoclimatology, Palaeoecology,* Vol. 290, 1–10.

Reichow, Marc K., et al. 2009. "The Timing and Extent of the Eruption of the Siberian Traps Large Igneous Province: Implications for the End-Permian Environmental Crisis." *Earth and Planetary Science Letters,* Vol. 277 (1–2), 9–20.

Roghi, Guido, Eugenio Ragazzi, and Piero Gianolla. 2006. "Triassic Amber of the Southern Alps (Italy)." *Palaios,* Vol. 21, 143–154.

Taylor, Edith L. and Thomas N. Taylor. 1993. "Fossil Tree Rings and Paleoclimate From the Triassic of Antarctica." *New Mexico Museum of Natural History and Science Bulletin,* No. 3, Vol. 295, Issues 1–2, 162–191.

Whiteside, Jessica H., et al. 2010. "Compound-Specific Carbon Isotopes From Earth's Largest Flood Basalt Eruptions Directly Linked to the End-Triassic Mass Extinction." *PNAS,* Vol. 107, No. 15, 6721–6725.

Wang, Xiaofeng, et al. 2008. "The Late Triassic Black Shales of the Guanling Area, Guizhou Province, South-West China: a Unique Marine Reptile and Pelagic Crinoid Fossil Lagerstätte." *Palaeontology,* Vol. 51 (1), 27–61.

WEBSITES

The International Commission on Stratigraphy, stratigraphy.org, is the source of the dates in the time lines. The Paleomap Project, scotese.com, and Ron Blakey's site, cpgeosystems.com, were the main sources for paleomaps.

Staff for This Book
Ariane Szu-Tu, *Project Editor*
David Seager, *Art Director*
Lori Epstein, *Senior Photo Editor*
Paige Towler, *Editorial Assistant*
Sanjida Rashid, *Design Production Assistant*
Michael Cassady, *Rights Clearance Specialist*
Grace Hill, *Managing Editor*
Joan Gossett, *Senior Production Editor*
Lewis R. Bassford, *Production Manager*
Rachel Faulise, *Manager, Production Services*
Susan Borke, *Legal and Business Affairs*

Published by the National Geographic Society
Gary E. Knell, *President and CEO*
John M. Fahey, *Chairman of the Board*
Melina Gerosa Bellows, *Chief Education Officer*
Declan Moore, *Chief Media Officer*
Hector Sierra, *Senior Vice President and General Manager, Book Division*

Senior Management Team, Kids Publishing and Media Nancy Laties Feresten, *Senior Vice President;* Jennifer Emmett, *Vice President, Editorial Director, Kids Books;* Julie Vosburgh Agnone, *Vice President, Editorial Operations;* Rachel Buchholz, *Editor and Vice President,* NG Kids *magazine;* Michelle Sullivan, *Vice President, Kids Digital;* Eva Absher-Schantz, *Design Director;* Jay Sumner, *Photo Director;* Hannah August, *Marketing Director;* R. Gary Colbert, *Production Director*

Digital Anne McCormack, *Director;* Laura Goertzel, Sara Zeglin, *Producers;* Jed Winer, *Special Projects Assistant;* Emma Rigney, *Creative Producer;* Brian Ford, *Video Producer;* Bianca Bowman, *Assistant Producer;* Natalie Jones, *Senior Product Manager*

The National Geographic Society is one of the world's largest nonprofit scientific and educational organizations. Founded in 1888 to "increase and diffuse geographic knowledge," the Society's mission is to inspire people to care about the planet. It reaches more than 400 million people worldwide each month through its official journal, *National Geographic,* and other magazines; National Geographic Channel; television documentaries; music; radio; films; books; DVDs; maps; exhibitions; live events; school publishing programs; interactive media; and merchandise. National Geographic has funded more than 10,000 scientific research, conservation, and exploration projects and supports an education program promoting geographic literacy.

For more information, please visit nationalgeographic.com, call 1-800-NGS LINE (647-5463), or write to the following address:
National Geographic Society
1145 17th Street N.W.
Washington, D.C. 20036-4688 U.S.A.

Visit us online at nationalgeographic.com/books

For librarians and teachers: ngchildrensbooks.org

More for kids from National Geographic: kids.nationalgeographic.com

For information about special discounts for bulk purchases, please contact National Geographic Books Special Sales: ngspecsales@ngs.org

For rights or permissions inquiries, please contact National Geographic Books Subsidiary Rights: ngbookrights@ngs.org

"Evolve or Perish" game, page 114, courtesy of the Smithsonian Institution.

Paperback ISBN: 978-1-4263-2104-7
Reinforced library binding ISBN: 978-1-4263-2105-4

Printed in Hong Kong
15/THK/1